United States
Department of
Agriculture

Forest Service

Pacific Northwest
Research Station

General Technical Report
PNW-GTR-849

February 2012

Gathering in the City: An Annotated Bibliography and Review of the Literature About Human-Plant Interactions in Urban Ecosystems

R.J. McLain, K. MacFarland, L. Brody, J. Hebert, P. Hurley, M. Poe, L.P. Buttolph, N. Gabriel, M. Dzuna, M.R. Emery, and S. Charnley

Authors

R.J. McLain, **L.P. Buttolph,** and **M. Poe** are social scientists, Institute for Culture and Ecology, P.O. Box 6688, Portland, OR 97228-6688; **K. MacFarland** and **J. Hebert** were student interns, Institute for Culture and Ecology; **N. Gabriel** is a Ph.D. candidate, Rutgers University, Department of Geography, Brunswick, NJ; **P. Hurley** is an assistant professor, Ursinus College in the Environmental Studies Program, Collegeville, PA 19426-1000; **L. Brody** and **M. Dzuna** were students, Ursinus College; **M.R. Emery** is a research geographer, U.S. Department of Agriculture, Forest Service, Northern Research Station, Burlington, VT 95403; **S. Charnley** is an environmental anthropologist, U.S. Department of Agriculture, Forest Service, Pacific Northwest Research Station, Forestry Sciences Laboratory, P.O. Box 3890, Portland, OR 97208.

Cover photographs by Melissa Poe.

Abstract

McLain, R.J.; MacFarland, K.; Brody, L.; Hebert, J.; Hurley, P.; Poe, M.; Buttolph, L.P.; Gabriel, N.; Dzuna, M.; Emery, M.R.; Charnley, S. 2012. Gathering in the city: an annotated bibliography and review of the literature about human-plant interactions in urban ecosystems. Gen. Tech. Rep. PNW-GTR-849. Portland, OR: U.S. Department of Agriculture, Forest Service, Pacific Northwest Research Station. 107 p.

The past decade has seen resurgence in interest in gathering wild plants and fungi in cities. In addition to gathering by individuals, dozens of groups have emerged in U.S., Canadian, and European cities to facilitate access to nontimber forest products (NTFPs), particularly fruits and nuts, in public and private spaces. Recent efforts within cities to encourage public orchards and food forests, and to incorporate more fruit and nut trees into street tree planting programs indicate a growing recognition among planners that gathering is an important urban activity. Yet the academic literature has little to say about urban gathering practices or the people who engage in them. This annotated bibliography and literature review is a step toward filling the gap in knowledge about the socioecological roles of NTFPs in urban ecosystems in the United States. Our objectives are to demonstrate that gathering—the collecting of food and raw materials—is a type of human-plant interaction that warrants greater attention in urban green space management, and to provide an overview of the literature on human-plant interactions—including gathering—in urban environments. Our review found that very few studies of urban gathering have been done. Consequently, we included gathering field guides, Web sites, and articles from the popular media in our search. These sources, together with the small number of scientific studies of urban gathering, indicated that people derive numerous benefits from gathering plants and fungi in U.S. cities. Gathering provides useful products, encourages physical activity, offers opportunities to connect with and learn about nature, helps strengthen social ties and cultural identities, and, in some contexts, can serve as a strategic tool for ecological restoration. These benefits parallel those identified in environmental psychology and cultural ecology studies of the effects of gardening and being in nature. The literature on human-plant interactions also emphasizes that humans need to be treated as endogenous factors in dynamic, socially and spatially heterogeneous urban ecosystems. Spatially explicit analyses of human-plant interactions show that the distribution of wealth and power within societies affects the composition, species distribution, and structure of urban ecologies. Our review also indicates that tensions exist between NTFP gatherers and land managers, as well as between gatherers and other citizens over gathering, particularly in public spaces. This tension likely is related to perceptions about the impact these practices have on cherished species and spaces. We conclude that gathering is an important urban activity and deserves a greater role in urban management given its social and potential ecological benefits. Research on urban gathering will require sensitivity to existing power imbalances and the use of theoretical frameworks and methodologies that assume humans are integral and not always negative components of ecosystems.

Keywords: Cultural practices, green infrastructure, nontimber forest products, urban foraging, urban gathering, urban forestry, urban planning.

Contents

Introduction

For much of humankind's history, the gathering of plants, fungi, mosses, lichens, and their parts was essential to individual and group survival. With the domestication of animals and plants, reliance on gathered products diminished but did not cease. The gathering of wild and semi-wild products remains an important economic activity around the world, directly providing food and medicine for many, as well as raw materials for pharmaceuticals, health and beauty products, crafts, and the food and beverage industries. Additionally, the literature on contemporary rural gathering in developed countries highlights the many noneconomic values associated with gathering, including development and transmission of ecological knowledge, recreational opportunities, mental and physical well-being, spiritual fulfillment, reinforcement of cultural identities, and strengthening of social ties.

In the United States, urban foresters have played a prominent role in persuading municipal governments of the importance of trees and green space in urban environments. They emphasize the benefits of urban vegetation, including better air quality, lower summer air temperatures, aesthetics, and improvements in psychological well-being. Rarely mentioned, however, are the numerous nontimber forest products (NTFPs), such as food, medicine, decorative materials, building materials, ornamental plants, and firewood, that are or could be gathered in urban ecosystems. Also unmentioned are the sociocultural, psychological, and physical fitness benefits people derive from taking part in gathering activities.

For example, gathering of wild mushrooms and plants allows immigrants from many cultures to obtain fruits, nuts, berries, and medicinal plants that remind them of their homelands. Gathering also provides opportunities for humans to connect with nature, allowing them to develop long-term relationships with particular types of plants or fungi and gathering sites. Gathering frequently involves developing ecological knowledge about where and how particular kinds of plants and fungi grow, and sharing that information with family, friends, and neighbors. Gathering also has many health benefits. It gives people a reason to get outdoors and be physically active; it also relieves stress and is a way for people to relax.

Despite the invisibility of gathering in urban forestry and planning discourse, a review of botanical field guides, news articles, and Web sites indicates that urban gathering is a geographically widespread practice in the contemporary United States. Individuals of diverse ethnic and racial backgrounds, age groups, and income levels participate in urban gathering. Additionally, the past decade has seen the emergence of dozens of formal groups dedicated to various forms of urban NTFP gathering. Among others, these groups include Fallen Fruit in Los Angeles, Urban Edibles in Portland, Oregon, the Philadelphia Orchard Project, and the

Iskash*taa program in Tucson, Arizona. The emergence of these groups strongly suggests that gathering is gaining greater visibility and popularity. Moreover, recent research in Japan (Kobori and Primack 2003) indicates that the harvesting of culturally valued products such as fuel wood or edible roots on a regular basis is essential for restoring habitats for some endangered wildlife species. Thus in addition to its social, cultural, and economic values, strategic encouragement of urban gathering may be an important tool for developing and maintaining ecologically sustainable ecosystems.

However, at present there is a dearth of scientific knowledge about gathering in urban ecosystems. Even very basic information, such as where gathering takes place, what products are gathered, who gathers them, and what motivates people to gather is nonexistent. Fields that strongly influence municipal vegetation management and open space policies, such as environmental psychology, urban forestry, urban ecology, and urban planning, are largely silent on the topic of urban gathering. Although gathering long predates activities such as gardening and tree planting, which are extensively researched by environmental psychologists and urban foresters, neither discipline examines how gathering in urban ecosystems affects individual or community well-being. Even the field of cultural ecology, with its long tradition of studying contemporary gathering practices in rural communities and more recent exploration of the cultural importance of gardens and yards in contemporary urban lives, has little to say about gathering in cities. Only very recently have restoration ecologists begun to envision integrating gathering activities into restoration programs. Likewise, ethnoecologists and political ecologists have just begun to turn their attention to studying the ways in which gatherers influence urban ecosystems and the ways in which urbanization processes affect gatherers.

Purpose

This annotated bibliography is intended for scholars, planners, and managers and seeks to address the gap in knowledge about the socioecological roles of gathering NTFPs in urban and periurban ecosystems in the United States, including impacts on biophysical components. We have documented through a review of the academic and popular literature that gathering persists and may be growing in U.S. cities, is of interest to people from many walks of life, and provides a wide range of benefits to gatherers and the communities in which they live. This bibliography also exposes planners, managers, and scientists to a range of approaches used to study human-plant relationships in urban environments. Our intention is to provide scientists and practitioners with a basic, albeit preliminary, knowledge of the social and ecological dimensions of urban gathering, as well as an introduction to the intellectual tools that could be applied to broadening our understanding of how urban gathering can be integrated into sustainable urban ecosystem planning and management strategies.

Scope

The materials included in this bibliography are drawn from the scientific and popular literature about gathering, human-plant interactions, and urban ecosystem dynamics in the United States, Canada, Europe, the United Kingdom, Australia, and New Zealand. Our initial search of the scientific literature yielded only a handful of articles on urban-based gatherers or gathering. We therefore reconceptualized our purpose as an effort to develop better understanding of the interactions between humans and plants, fungi, mosses, and lichens in urban ecosystems, with gathering being a subset of such interactions. For the sake of brevity, we use the term plants to encompass these diverse organisms.

This wide-angle approach led us to examine the literature in the fields of urban ethnoecology, cultural ecology, political ecology, urban ecology, urban forestry, environmental psychology, urban planning, and environmental health. Each of these areas of study speaks to some aspect of urban gathering, although few researchers in these fields examine urban gathering practices directly. For example, urban ecologists and urban foresters describe the biophysical dynamics that underlie specific types of ecological structures and processes, which in turn affect which plants and fungi are available to urban gatherers. Political ecologists show how social structures and distributions of power shape urban ecologies, as well as who has access to specific types of urban vegetation. Environmental psychologists, as well as some urban foresters, examine the effects of human interactions with vegetation on individual health and community well-being. Cultural and political ecologists document how individual and group identities both shape and are shaped by garden and yard ecologies. Ethnoecologists, a subset of cultural ecologists, explore how ecological knowledge is produced and passed on; they also document the uses that humans make of plants. Environmental health scientists provide information about the presence and distribution of toxic and beneficial elements in soil, air, and water, factors that potentially influence the health risks and benefits associated with the use of plant products originating in urban environments. Urban planners provide understanding of the institutional frameworks within which these activities take place, as well as ideas for ecologically sustainable urban designs.

Additionally, we reviewed key articles on contemporary rural gathering, a topic that crosses many of the disciplines, fields, and subfields mentioned above. Foraging field guides were also included in the review as they provide important insights about the species present in U.S. cities as well as information about actual and recommended gathering practices. We supplemented our review of the scientific literature and field guides with a sampling of articles from major news publications, Web sites, and blogs related to urban gathering.

Because of time constraints, we were unable to review planning ordinances, laws pertaining to urban trees and vegetation, and arborist trade journals. However, we recognize the critical importance of such an endeavor in future research on urban gathering.

Definitions

Studies of urban NTFP gathering are complicated by the slipperiness of the terms, "urban," "NTFP," and "gathering." Additionally the term "urban forest" is challenging to define. A brief explanation of how we use each of these terms is provided below.

Nontimber forest products—

There is no single widely used term for the plants, fungi, and other botanical products that humans gather in forested environments. Professional foresters currently use a number of terms to refer to these products (Belcher et al. 2003), including nontimber forest products, special forest products, alternative forest products, minor forest products, and nonwood forest products. Of these terms, "nontimber forest products" is the most widely used in academic publications and is also in common use among land management agencies in many parts of the world. We use this term throughout this publication. We define NTFPs broadly to include entire plants, plant parts (e.g., seeds, cones, leaves, branches, flowers, fruits, and nuts), plant exudates (i.e., resin, sap, and oils), fungi, mosses, and lichens. Following international convention, we also include wood products such as firewood, poles, and specialty woods for crafts.

Gathering—

There is no single term for the activities categorized in this document as "gathering." Other terms commonly used for these activities include foraging, collecting, harvesting, gleaning, picking, and, depending on the product, tapping or digging. All of these activities involve the removal of fungi, plants, or parts of plants from where they are either growing (in the case of live plants) or where they have fallen or been transported by natural forces.

An important question that surfaces repeatedly with the concept of "gathering" is how it differs from gardening or other forms of cultivation. Ford (1985) described a continuum of human-plant production interactions with foraging on one end, cultivation in the middle, and domestication on the other end. Ethnobotanists also often include the category of "tending" between foraging and cultivation. The following passage from Deur (2002: 12–13) clarifies the distinctions between tending, cultivation, and domestication.

> Plant "tending," most scholars now agree, involves the minor modification of environments to encourage the growth of naturally occurring plants in situ, while plant "cultivation" involves a more intensive and extensive pattern of environmental modification. Cultivation, as it is now commonly defined, involves the seeding or transplanting of propagules, the intentional fertilization or modification of soils, improvements of irrigation or drainage, and the clearing or "weeding" of competing plants. "Domestication," by contrast, involves the genetic modification of crops, likely resulting from the selective cultivation of plants with anomalous and desirable traits.

The boundaries between tending and foraging, however, are fuzzy, as are the boundaries between each of the other categories. Additionally, the particularities of urban environments, such as a high percentage of exotic species relative to native species and the presence of numerous and abundant naturalized domesticates make the use of Ford's continuum problematic as a descriptor of human-plant production interactions in cities. A further complication in cities is that urban gatherers are highly likely to harvest products from plants cultivated or tended by others (including species that are legacies of historic management regimes), with or without the cultivator's or tender's knowledge or permission.

To address these problems, we have modified Ford's continuum to fit contemporary urban environments, drawing on the admittedly limited data available on urban gathering (see fig. 1). Our diagram represents the continuum from gatherer to plant tender to cultivator, as in urban areas, it is likely that many people harvest products from vegetation that are cultivated—albeit often by someone other than the gatherer. We have included examples of activities at different points along the continuum to give readers a sense of the people we would classify as gatherers, plant tenders, and cultivators. We see this continuum as a starting point for discussion and expect that it will be modified or replaced entirely as understandings of urban gathering practices increase.

Urban and periurban areas—
We look at the literature on gathering in both urban and periurban areas. We use the 2010 U.S. Census' definition of urban areas, which is land area consisting of "densely developed territory, and encompass[ing] residential, commercial, and other non-residential urban land uses." Periurban areas are defined as "regions adjacent to urban areas and clearly under their influence" (Konijnendijk et al. 2006: 9).

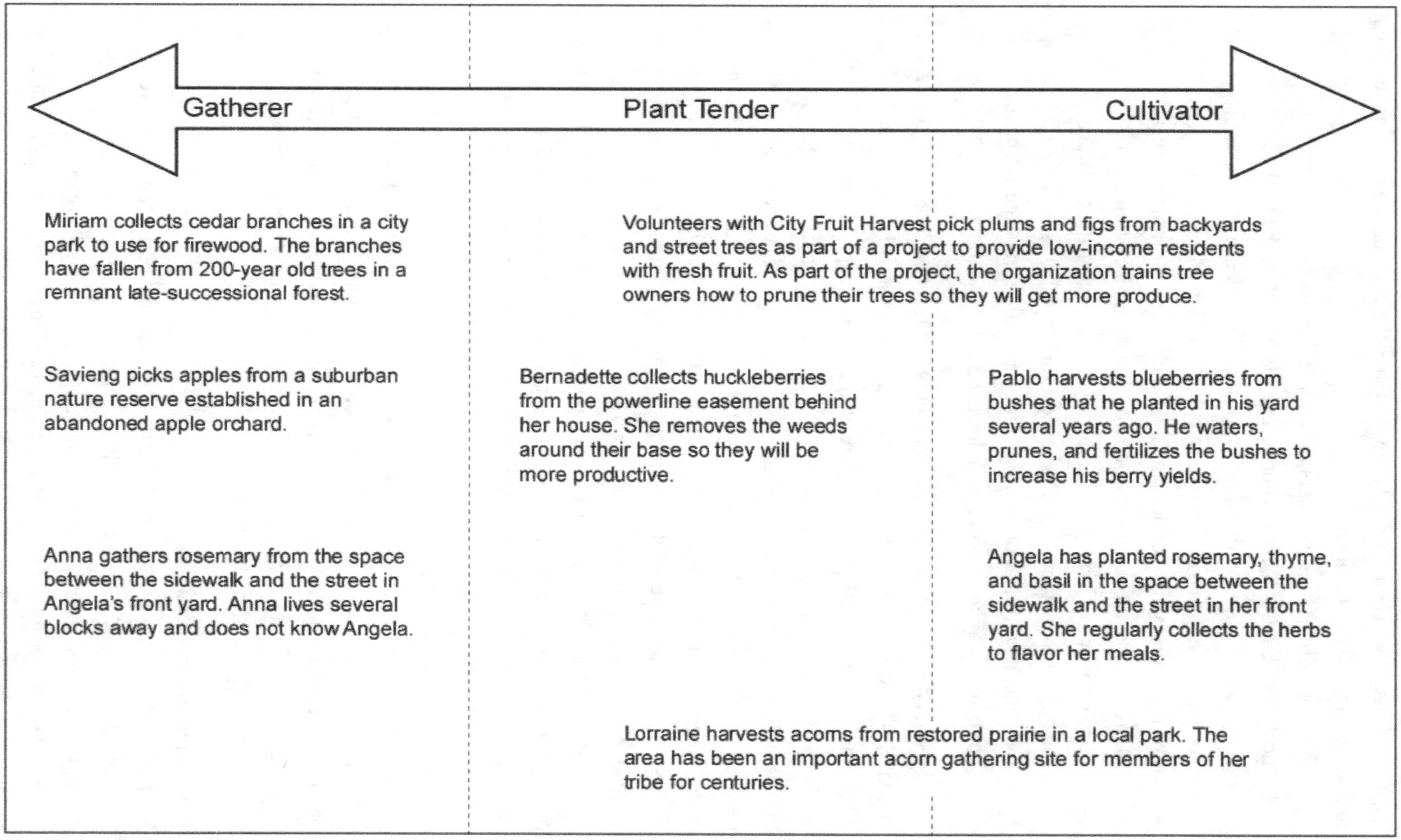

Gatherer — Plant Tender — Cultivator

Gatherer

Miriam collects cedar branches in a city park to use for firewood. The branches have fallen from 200-year old trees in a remnant late-successional forest.

Savieng picks apples from a suburban nature reserve established in an abandoned apple orchard.

Anna gathers rosemary from the space between the sidewalk and the street in Angela's front yard. Anna lives several blocks away and does not know Angela.

Plant Tender

Volunteers with City Fruit Harvest pick plums and figs from backyards and street trees as part of a project to provide low-income residents with fresh fruit. As part of the project, the organization trains tree owners how to prune their trees so they will get more produce.

Bernadette collects huckleberries from the powerline easement behind her house. She removes the weeds around their base so they will be more productive.

Lorraine harvests acorns from restored prairie in a local park. The area has been an important acorn gathering site for members of her tribe for centuries.

Cultivator

Pablo harvests blueberries from bushes that he planted in his yard several years ago. He waters, prunes, and fertilizes the bushes to increase his berry yields.

Angela has planted rosemary, thyme, and basil in the space between the sidewalk and the street in her front yard. She regularly collects the herbs to flavor her meals.

Figure 1—Activities along the gatherer–cultivator continuum.

Urban forest–

The 1978 Cooperative Forestry Assistance Act for the United States defines urban forestry as "the planning, establishment, protection, and management of trees and associated plants, individually, in small groups, or under forest conditions within cities, their suburbs, and towns." Following this definition, the urban forest includes all trees and associated vegetation in urban and periurban areas. Trees and associated plants in private yards, as well as trees located along streets, in parking lots or stormwater management features, and in other green spaces (e.g., parks and institutional grounds) are considered part of the urban forest. Exotic fruit and nut-bearing trees, including those commonly thought of as orchard trees (i.e., cherry, apple, and peach trees) are also elements of urban forests.

Organization of Materials

We have organized the bibliography into three major sections—"Key Findings," "Gathering Literature and Web Resources," and "Academic Literature." Because of the large amount of bibliographic material, we have placed the "Key Findings" section first. Along with highlighting the key themes identified through synthesizing the many sets of literature pertinent to urban gathering, the "Key Findings" section suggests next steps for future research and discusses key challenges associated with research on urban gathering.

The second major section includes annotated citations of literature that is specifically related to gathering and is divided into the following topics:

- Academic literature on urban gathering, including research in urban ethnoecology
- Academic literature on gathering in rural areas
- Field guides for gatherers
- Popular news articles
- Web sites related to urban gathering

The third section consists of academic literature drawn from areas of research with significant potential to inform studies of urban gathering conceptually or methodologically and is divided into the following topics:

- Cultural ecology
- Political ecology
- Environmental psychology
- Urban forestry
- Urban ecology
- Environmental health
- Urban planning

Cultural ecology, political ecology, and environmental psychology tend to focus on the human side of human-plant interactions, whereas urban forestry, urban ecology, and environmental health emphasize the plant side. Urban planning is where the two aspects of human-plant interaction come together in on-the-ground practice. Table 1 summarizes the kinds of topics relevant to human-plant interactions that are the focus of each of these fields. Because much of the research on the topic of human-plant interactions is interdisciplinary, a number of the articles overlap two or more fields of study. Additionally, many of the articles cover multiple topics of relevance to urban gathering. To help readers identify articles relevant to a particular topic of interest or field of study, we have numbered the annotations in consecutive order and included keywords after each annotation. The appendix provides a list of all keywords and the number for each article associated with that keyword.

Table 1—Primary research topics covered by human-plant interaction studies

Research topics	CE	PE	EP	EH	UE	UF	UP
Influence of human-plant interactions on mental health	X	X	X			X	X
Influence of human-plant interaction on physical health	X			X			X
Influence of human-plant interactions on community well-being		X	X			X	X
Social distribution of environmental benefits and costs associated with vegetation management		X			X		X
Links between vegetation and individual identities	X	X	X				
Links between vegetation and cultural identities	X	X	X			X	
Human uses of urban forest products	X	X					
Urban forest assessments and valuations						X	
Acquisition and transmission of ecological knowledge	X	X					
Urban forest tenure regimes		X					X
Differential access to urban forest products		X					
Differences in species preferences, attitudes, and values	X	X	X			X	X
Urban forest biophysical conditions and characteristics		X		X	X	X	X
Spatial distribution of vegetation		X		X	X	X	X
Impacts of human activities on ecological conditions	X	X		X	X	X	X

CE = Cultural ecology (includes ethnoecology).
PE = Political ecology (overlaps with CE).
EP = Environmental psychology.
EH = Environmental health.
UE = Urban ecology.
UF = Urban forestry (overlaps with EP and UE).
UP = Urban Planning (some overlap with EP).

References Cited in Introduction

Belcher, B.M. 2003. What isn't an NTFP? International Forestry Review. 5(2): 161–168.

Cooperative Forestry Assistance Act of 1978; 16 U.S.C. Chapter 41 Section 2109.

Deur, D. 2002. Plant cultivation on the northwest coast: a reconsideration. Journal of Cultural Geography. 19(2): 9–35.

Ford, R.I. 1985. The processes of plant food production in prehistoric North America. In: Ford, R.I., ed. Prehistoric food production in North America. Anthropological Papers Number 75. Ann Arbor, MI: Museum of Anthropology, University of Michigan: 1–18.

Kobori, H.; Primack, R.B. 2003. Participatory conservation approaches for satoyama, the traditional forest and agricultural landscape of Japan. Ambio. 32(4): 307–311.

Konijnendijk, C.C.; Ricard, R.M.; Kenney, A.; Randrup, T.B. 2006. Defining urban forestry—a comparative perspective of North America and Europe. Urban Forestry and Urban Greening. 4(3-4): 93–103.

U.S. Census Bureau. 2010. 2010 Census urban and rural classification and urban area criteria. http://www.census.gov/geo/www/ua/2010urbanruralclass.html. (November 13, 2010).

Key Findings

Our review of the literature and Web resources related to gathering indicates that gathering is a multifaceted, dynamic human practice that has much to contribute toward efforts to develop sustainable urban ecosystems. This section summarizes our key findings, suggests next steps for future urban gathering research, and discusses the major challenges that managers and researchers will face when implementing urban gathering studies.

1. Cities are dynamic, spatially and socially heterogeneous socioecological systems in which humans are most accurately viewed as embedded, rather than separate, components.

In the past decade, both social and natural scientists have converged on the notion that humans need to be treated as endogenous factors in urban ecosystems. Urban ecologists emphasize the spatial heterogeneity of these systems, whereas political and cultural ecologists draw attention to their social heterogeneity. Spatially explicit analyses of human-plant interactions by both political and urban ecologists show that the distribution of wealth and power within societies affects the composition, species distribution, and structure of urban ecosystems. These characteristics of urban socioecological systems suggest important directions for research on urban nontimber forest products (NTFPs) gathering practices. One key question to ask is, "How does social heterogeneity in urban ecosystems, including the heterogeneity of gatherers themselves, affect heterogeneity in the biophysical attributes of those systems?" A second important question is, "How does patchiness of the biophysical system condition gathering practices, including the social relations in which they are embedded?"

2. Interacting with plants significantly affects individual and community health and well-being.

A large body of evidence shows that being in the presence of plants and interacting with plants tactilely affect mood, stress levels, self-esteem, and ability to focus. Gathering promotes the physical and mental health benefits associated with active pursuits in the outdoors. Gathering can also increase connections to traditional foodways and healing practices, improving nutrition and reducing diabetes and stress-related illnesses. Additionally, the presence of vegetation can affect crime rates and social interaction. Often these influences are positive, but in some contexts, "messy" vegetation can signify that a place is dangerous or insecure. However, what constitutes "messy" vegetation is heavily influenced by cultural and neighborhood norms so that one person's "messy" landscape might seem orderly to someone else. Plants also function as an important medium through which both individual and collective identities, values, and norms are developed and maintained. This has ecological consequences, as efforts to assert individual and cultural identities influence what species people choose to plant or retain, their use of fertilizers and herbicides, and the "messiness" of the vegetation on their properties. However, environmental health research shows that there are also potential physical health risks from consuming plants or fungi grown on contaminated soils or in heavily polluted areas. Accurately assessing those risks is a complex undertaking as species differ greatly in their uptake of contaminants and the parts in which contaminants are stored also differ, as does the spatial distribution of contaminants across city landscapes. Research on the health and safety aspect of urban gathering will help clarify potential contributions to policy considerations such as food security and public health.

3. Gatherers come from a diversity of sociocultural backgrounds.

The evidence suggests that gathering, whether rural or urban, is an activity that cuts across divisions of age, gender, education, class, race, and ethnicity. By this we do not mean to say that there are no differences along these divisions in terms of numbers of practitioners, kinds of products gathered, harvesting methods, locations of gathering sites, or motivations for gathering. Indeed, we strongly suspect that such differences exist. Yet at the same time, it is important for scientists, planners, and managers to recognize that gathering is a form of practice (Robbins et al. 2008) and that gatherers come from diverse backgrounds and thus likely differ in their motivations for gathering, the kinds of products they gather, the depth of their ecological knowledge, and the techniques they use for gathering plants and fungi. Two key take-home messages for policymakers seeking to regulate gathering are that one-size-fits-all policies are likely to be both unpopular and ineffective and that developing effective and enforceable policies will require gaining the trust and involvement of a broad spectrum of people.

4. People participate in urban gathering for a variety of reasons.

People gather plants in cities for many reasons. Some people gather plants to obtain foods or medicinal products that they cannot easily obtain in local stores or afford to buy. Others gather as a way to learn about the world around them, a reason to spend time outside, and an essential component of their quality of life. For some people, gathering is a long-standing family or cultural tradition, a conduit for intergenerational learning and transmission of local ecological knowledge, and a means for stewarding local and native plant populations. For still others, gathering is a means to earn income, whether as someone who teaches others how to forage or as a seller of harvested products. This diversity in motivations for gathering calls for policies and management strategies that are flexible and tailored to specific contexts.

5. Urban gathering encompasses a diversity of species and products.

Preliminary research indicates that a large number of species and products are gathered in urban ecosystems. Jahnige (2002) recorded 103 products gathered from 78 species in Baltimore; Gabriel (2006) documented 74 products gathered from 70 species in Philadelphia. The field guides annotated in this volume describe hundreds of plants and products that people gather, including many that are found in urban or periurban areas. The heterogeneity of species and products harvested argues for policymakers to avoid simplistic one-size-fits-all approaches, such as blanket prohibitions on all gathering in public spaces. Instead, gathering regulations should take into account the species, product, and socioecological context in which these activities take place.

6. Land and resource tenure issues associated with urban gathering are complex.

Tensions and questions over rights of access to gathering sites are common in rural areas, particularly where landowners recently have prohibited or restricted access to sites that previously were open to harvesters. In many U.S. cities, gathering challenges the sharp distinctions commonly drawn between public and private property. This is especially true for quasipublic spaces, such as vegetated strips between sidewalks and streets, where tenure is vague and enforcement of private or public claims to fruit, nuts, leaves, and other plant parts is costly. In some cases, areas that have historically been treated as neighborhood commons or de facto open access sites, such as vacant lots and woodlands, recently have shifted into commercial or residential use and access to NTFPs on those lands has become more restricted. In other areas, abandoned properties are being transformed into new de facto commons or open access. Knowledge of existing tenure regimes and how they are influenced by changes in land use and ownership is fundamental to understanding how policies affect different types of gatherers and their gathering practices.

7. Land use policies and management activities can have both negative and positive effects on urban gathering and gatherers.

Relationships between gathering and land use policies and management are complex. Some land use policies, such as efforts to restore native vegetation in urban green spaces, could result in decreased access to valued exotic species that previously were gathered in those areas. At the same time, such efforts could increase access to products obtained from native species, provided that people are permitted to gather such products in those spaces. Species that are important to gatherers also may proliferate with urban expansion and suburban land management practices. Both negative and positive effects are associated with land use legacies. For example, vacant lots in deindustrializing areas of some cities can become spaces where people harvest plants; however, in some cases, residual toxic chemicals in the soil may pose health risks for consumers of gathered products.

8. Gathering can have both negative and positive impacts on urban ecosystems.

Many parks and open spaces prohibit gathering, and preliminary indications are that land managers hold diverse views about whether gathering has a negative impact on urban ecosystems. Many default to a stance that it does, while others may be more open to some collecting practices and harvest of specific target species. Documented evidence that gathering negatively affects urban ecologies is nonexistent. However, it is reasonable to assume that some types of gathering practices, such as the removal of whole plants or roots, might reduce desired plant (or indirectly animal) populations in urban environments. But human gathering practices could equally well have positive impacts on urban plant populations, and gatherers often perceive their activities in terms of environmental stewardship, employing a system of ethical norms in their gathering practices and sometimes directly tending to species and habitat health. The relative ecosystem impacts of gathering requires further examination that attends to both dispersed and intensive gathering techniques on specific plant and fungi. Researchers and planners might also contrast gathering with the impacts of other land uses, such as industrial development and commercial agriculture. From the standpoint of the social environment, the presence of gatherers in urban parks and vacant lots potentially supports the development of informal surveillance networks that can reduce crime rates and increase perceptions of public safety.

9. Research on urban gathering requires sensitivity to existing power imbalances and the use of theoretical frameworks and methodologies that assume humans are integral (and not always negative) components of ecosystems.

Urban gathering is largely a decentralized activity practiced by disparate individuals and organizations, with little to no municipal support or involvement. Decentralization coupled with low visibility allows gatherers to engage in practices that are often neither fully legal nor illegal. Indeed, they **may** be invisible to government officials, land managers, park users, landowners, and neighbors. However, this decentralization makes understanding urban gathering and identifying ways for urban planning and management efforts to support sustainable gathering practices more difficult. Interdisciplinary, participatory, and mixed-methods research approaches are needed to understand the complexities of urban gathering, the political ecologies that support gathering, and the people who participate in it.

Next Steps

The potential social and ecological benefits of urban gathering studies are numerous. Data from such studies would contribute to:

- Urban NTFP management practices to maintain and enhance gathered species and associated habitats
- Efforts by "green" planners and urban food policy councils to reintegrate livelihood uses into urban green spaces
- Food security programs aimed at improving access of low-income populations to fresh fruits and nuts
- Public health programs aimed at reducing obesity and associated risks such as diabetes
- Programs such as the U.S. Forest Service's More Kids in the Woods initiative that aim to connect people, especially children, to nature in urban environments
- Efforts to improve the ecological literacy of urban populations
- Social and cultural traditions that revolve around gathering by urban residents

However, realizing these benefits requires support for research that draws on and integrates methods and theories from both the natural and social sciences. Future research will therefore need to address the following considerations.

1. Integrate studies of gathering into ongoing urban ecosystem research

An overwhelming conclusion from reading the literature on human-plant interactions in contemporary urban ecosystems in the second half of this document is that gatherers and gathering are strikingly absent from view. Does this silence reflect a lack of gathering activity taking place in cities? The news articles, Web sites, gathering field guides, and the handful of scientific articles included in the following sections of this document suggest otherwise and argue for research to fill the gap in scientific knowledge about urban gathering.

A critical first step to address this gap is to integrate studies of gatherers and gathering practices into on-going urban ecosystem research. One approach is to develop gathering research that parallels studies that have already been done on other types of human-plant interactions. For example, environmental psychologists have documented at length the effects that activities such as gardening, walking or being in wooded areas, and participation in tree-planting programs have on people's moods, sense of self, and levels of stress. Similarly, cultural ecologists have conducted numerous studies that show how gardens and gardening challenge binary categorizations of the world. Parallel studies of gathering that draw on the conceptual frameworks and methodologies used in these studies would help round out scientific understandings of human-plant interactions. A second approach is to include questions about gathering in new research where appropriate. For example, an urban planner doing a comparative study of stewardship activities in different neighborhoods might investigate whether gatherers in those areas conceptualize their activities as a form of stewardship. The new national system of Urban Long Term Research Areas for integrated social and ecological research on urban ecosystems provides an excellent framework for integrating gathering research into broader urban ecosystem studies.

2. Develop a holistic research program focused on gathering

Also needed are studies that focus specifically on gathering as an everyday practice in urban ecosystems. These would provide extensive and detailed looks at the world(s) of urban gathering and would complement the integrative studies described above. Such studies would address urban ecologists' concerns with understanding the "who, what, when, how, why, and where" of human activities in cities (Grove and Burch 1997: 269). They would also address political ecologists' concern for understanding how the distribution of power influences human-environment interactions. The following aspects of gathering would be important to include in the initial phases of such research.

- The different types of gathering practices utilized

- The diversity of species and products gathered

- Demographic characteristics of the individuals who engage in gathering

- Motivations for gathering

- How people use gathered products

- The economic, social, and cultural importance of gathering and gathered products to individuals, households, and communities

- Where gathering and gathered products occur and the attributes of these spaces, including land cover types, land uses and history, and property regimes

- How gathering and gathering practices complement or conflict with existing ecosystem management and planning institutions (e.g., regulations) and activities (e.g., restoration and tree-planting programs)

Once these basic data have been collected, research targeting particular issues or concerns can be conducted, such as studies examining the ecological impacts of specific gathering practices on a particular species, the relationship between spatial ecology and access to valued species by diverse gatherers, or the comparative ethnoecological systems in urban nature, including the role of social media in the creation and transmission of gathering knowledge.

Challenges to Urban Gathering Research

Integrating gathering into urban ecosystem research, management, and planning will require overcoming two major challenges. One challenge is the everyday nature of gathering, particularly in its noncommercial forms, which Robbins et al. (2008) argued has made it easy for academicians to overlook and methodologically difficult to study. This challenge has diminished somewhat with the recent emergence of widespread interest in developing urban food production systems, including programs that emphasize the establishment of public orchards and edible streetscapes. The focus on edible landscapes, however, carries with it the risk that the gathering of nonedibles and noncultivars will continue to be marginalized. Qualitative social science methods are particularly well suited for studying the quotidian and less visible aspects of gathering as an urban practice. Another challenge is the "museumification" of nature (Gobster 2007) trend in which humans' opportunities for tactile interactions with nature are increasingly restricted that dominates green space management and planning. Overcoming this challenge will require demonstrating the positive, as well as negative, impacts that gathering activities can have on urban ecological systems, and shifting toward a paradigm that envisions urban nature as a place inhabited by people. Recent efforts to reintegrate the gathering of bamboo and bamboo shoots into restoration programs for Japan's satoyama forests (Kobori and Primack 2003, Terada et al. 2010) provide a model for how gatherers can support ecologically sound green space management. A network of similar action-research projects for U.S. urban ecological restoration programs has the potential to provide both social and ecological benefits to a broad spectrum of urban inhabitants.

References Cited in Key Findings

Gabriel, N. 2006. Urban non-timber forest products in Philadelphia. Philadelphia, PA: Temple University. 89 p. M.S. thesis.

Gobster, P. 2007. Urban park restoration and the "museumification" of nature. Nature and Culture. 2(2): 96–114.

Grove, J.M.; Burch, W.R., Jr. 1997. A social ecology approach and applications of urban ecosystem and landscape analyses: a case study of Baltimore, MD. Urban Ecosystems. 1: 259–275.

Jahnige, P. 2002. The hidden bounty of the urban forest. In: Jones, E.T.; McLain, R.J.; Weigand, J.F., eds. Nontimber forest products in the United States. Lawrence, KS: University of Kansas Press: 96–101.

Kobori, H.; Primack, R.B. 2003. Participatory conservation approaches for satoyama, the traditional forest and agricultural landscape of Japan. Ambio. 32(4): 307–311.

Robbins, P.; Emery, M.; Rice, J.L. 2008. Gathering in Thoreau's backyard: nontimber forest product harvesting as a practice. Area. 40(2): 265–277.

Terada, T.; Yokohari, M.; Bolthouse, J.; Tanaka, N. 2010. "Refueling" satoyama woodland restoration in Japan: enhancing restoration practice and experiences through woodfuel utilization. Nature and Culture. 5(3): 251–276.

Gathering Literature

This section includes annotations drawn from the academic literature on urban gathering, urban ethnoecology, and rural gathering. Field guides for wild plant and fungi gatherers, as well as articles in the popular media and Web sites for projects related to urban gathering also provide a wealth of information on gathering practices and gatherers. They also provide information that can serve as a foundation for integrating urban gathering into sustainable urban ecosystem management strategies. Additionally, the Internet and Web 2.0 technologies appear to be key communication and organizing tools for many urban gatherers.

Over the past two decades, a body of literature focused on contemporary nontimber forest products (NTFPs) gathering in countries of the global North has emerged. Scholars of contemporary gathering work in a variety of fields including anthropology, geography, sociology, rural sociology, social anthropology, cultural geography, environmental studies, and forestry. Most contemporary gathering research looks at gathering in rural areas; only a handful of studies examine NTFP gathering in urban or periurban settings. The emerging field of urban ethnoecology sheds light on urban gatherers and their practices in a few cities in the United States, the United Kingdom, and New Zealand. Studies of rural gathering suggest methods, approaches, and conceptual frameworks that are likely to be applicable in urban contexts as well.

Urban Gathering

The topic of contemporary urban gathering in countries of the global North has received little scholarly attention over the past century. However, in the past decade, a handful of scholars have published results drawn from studies of gathering in cities such as Baltimore (Jahnige 2002), Philadelphia (Gabriel 2006), and in periurban Charleston, South Carolina (Hurley et al. 2008, 2010). These studies suggest that the number of species and products harvested in urban and periurban settings is large. They also indicate that people from all walks of life gather plants and fungi in the city, and that people's motivations for gathering are diverse. Additionally, urban gathering sites are ecologically heterogeneous, ranging from sidewalk strips in residential developments to vacant lots to large public parks. Resource access is a key issue for gatherers and is conditioned by historical and present-day vegetation management policies and land use practices, as well as by public and private rules governing vegetation removal.

Konijnendijk et al.'s (2006) chapter on the importance of urban forests in Europe over time as sources of products such as firewood, game, mushrooms, fruits, and berries serves as a reminder that gathering in cities is a very old practice rather than something entirely new. In contrast, Nordahl's Public Produce (2009) focused on new forms of urban gathering, such as fruit mapping and backyard fruit gleaning, both of which have recently begun to be practiced in the United States and may be linked to wider food movements. Additionally, Nordahl argued for planners to rethink the ways in which public green space is used and managed. He further suggested that policies encouraging urban gathering, such as fruit and nut tree plantings along streets and in public parks, are important elements of sustainable urban ecosystems.

Ethnoecologists also recently have turned their attention to studies of plant and mushroom knowledge and practices in urban areas. A few of these studies have examined the linkages between migration, environmental knowledge, and cultural identity, suggesting that recent immigrants to urban, postindustrial places maintain connections to their cultural practices and form new social networks through ongoing uses of important plant materials (Balick et al. 2000, Ceuterick et al. 2008, Hodges and Bennett 2006). However, the plant material in these studies is frequently imported from areas outside the new urban context rather than gathered locally inside urban areas. Finally, one study (Wehi and Wehi 2009) of traditional plant harvesting in urban landscapes in New Zealand noted that urban public areas may be more important than nonurban areas for accessing important plants. This study also found that not only was urban gathering vitally important for supporting the maintenance of cultural practices and identities of people in urban areas (particularly indigenous people who may have been dislocated from their traditional resources areas), but that gathering was also positively correlated with ecosystem stewardship and biodiversity conservation. Studies of urban gathering indicate that ethnographies, user group surveys, and grounded theory are useful methods for urban gathering research. Additionally, Hurley et al. (2008) demonstrated the importance of including spatial analyses in urban gathering research toolkits.

1. Balick, M.; Kronenberg, F.; Ososki, A.L.; Reiff, M.; Fugh-Berman, A.; O'Connor, B.; Roble, M.; Lohr, P.; Atha, D. 2000. Medicinal plants used by Latino healers for women's health conditions in New York City. Economic Botany. 54(3): 344-357.

Discusses the use of plants by Latino healers in New York City to treat women's health. The authors interviewed eight Latino healers from the Dominican Republic and Puerto Rico who have been practicing traditional medicine in the United States between 3 to 51 years to identify the range and frequency of medicinal plants used to treat women and the methods used to collect medicinal plants. Sixty-seven plants were prescribed by the healers in this study and were administered as teas, aromatherapy, baths, herbs, rinses, and through ritual and dietary methods. Most plants were acquired through neighborhood herb shops, or **Botanicas**, and availability of traditional healing plants was presented as somewhat of a challenge. Four healers collected a few plant parts (leaves, flowers, roots) in New York City. They used specific knowledge to determine the timing (time of day, moon phase, etc.) to collect for best healing results, suggesting that traditional plant harvesting knowledge has been retained by these healers. The authors concluded by stating that ongoing use of traditional healing through plants by Latino immigrants has played a role in maintaining cultural ties and that the dynamic exchange of medicinal plants and knowledge give richness and complexity to urban ethnobotany and the study of people-plant relationships.

Keywords: Cultural practices, ethnobotany, ethnoecology, ethnomedicine, human health, immigrants, medicinal plants, urban gathering.

2. Ceuterick, M.I.V.; Torry, B.; Pieroni, A. 2008. Cross-cultural adaptation in urban ethnobotany: the Colombian folk pharmacopoeia in London. Journal of Ethnopharmacology. 120: 342–359.

The study, which took place in London between 2005 and 2007, documents the extent to which Colombian migrants have maintained traditional health care practices and the extent to which traditional knowledge and practices have been lost and new knowledge has been incorporated into health care practices. Twenty-three individuals of Colombian descent between 18 and 78 years old were included in the study. Data were gathered through semistructured interviews conducted in Spanish by using a snowball sampling strategy. Participants listed 46 species used in the treatment of 53 ailments and including 108 different uses. The authors found evidence of deculturation, with traditional treatments requiring fresh plant material tending to be abandoned and replaced with treatments based on plants more easily acquired in London. Treatments for conditions that occurred frequently in Colombia but rarely in London were also abandoned. Many of the plants used in migrant herbal remedies were purchased or sent by relatives still in Colombia. However, interviewees also obtained common plants, such as parsley, sage, lemon balm, aloe, and eucalyptus, from their own homes. The authors concluded that cross-cultural adaption of traditional health practices in cities like London needs to be understood as a multifaceted, multicultural process with both utilitarian and symbolic-cultural aspects.

Keywords: Cultural practices, ethnobotany, ethnoecology, ethnomedicine, human health, identity, immigrants, medicinal plants, urban gathering.

3. Gabriel, N. 2006. Urban non-timber forest products in Philadelphia. Philadelphia, PA: Temple University. 89 p. M.S. thesis.

Gabriel used a political ecology framework to explore how park policies favoring native ecosystem restoration in Philadelphia have affected gatherers and gathering activities in the city's parks. He carried out semistructured interviews with eight gatherers, supplementing these data with information obtained by interviewing park employees, horticultural society members, and individuals associated with other conservation-oriented organizations. The gatherers reported using more than 70 species of plants, evenly divided between native and nonnative species. The majority of interviewees gathered products for personal use or to share with others. Gathering was a source of food, medicine, and craft material; a form of recreation; a means for connecting with and learning about nature; and a way to share ecological knowledge. Most of the interviewees preferred to gather in large parks because they were less likely to be noticed by park officials or other park users. Vacant lots were infrequently used as gathering sites because of concerns about toxins from contaminated soils. Gabriel argued that involving nontimber forest product gatherers in park planning could be mutually beneficial as many gatherers develop specific and very detailed ecological knowledge in the course of their harvesting activities.

Keywords: Cultural practices, ecological knowledge, human health, policy, stewardship, urban gathering, urban planning, urban political ecology.

4. Hodges, S.; Bennett, B.C. 2006. The ethnobotany of Pluchea carolinensis (Jacq.) G. Don (Asteraceae) in the botánicas of Miami, Florida. Economic Botany. 60(1): 75–84.

Examines the uses of the plant *Pluchea carolinensis* (Jacq.) G. Don (commonly known as **salvia** and **la choige**) by Cuban and Haitian immigrant populations in southern Florida. *Pluchea carolinensis* is a shrub that grows naturally throughout the West Indies and from Mexico to northern parts of South America. The leaves of the plant are used medicinally and ritually for a wide range of ailments and spiritual practices. The researchers interviewed owners and employees at 27 **botanicas** (herbal shops) in north and south Miami. Seven of the **botanicas** served Haitian immigrants, and 20 served Latino immigrants. Research questions addressed plant identification, medicinal uses, ailments plant is used for, plant form, and method used to obtain the plant. Employees at 22 of the **botanicas** recognized the plant; two Haitian shops claimed they did not recognize the plant. Sixteen of the **botanicas** had *P. carolinensis* in stock at the time of the interview. Sources for the plant material included purchasing, growing in nurseries, or wild collecting. Employees at one Haitian store stated that *P. carolinensis* is easily found growing wild in disturbed areas around Miami. The authors considered employees at **botanicas** as urban ethnobotanical specialists, i.e., specialists who hold specific rather than generalized plant knowledge, and who acquire such knowledge in urban settings through both oral and written transmission. The authors concluded that **botanicas** in southern

Florida are important sources of ethnomedicinal knowledge and play a significant role in the region's health care system. This paper is relevant to urban nontimber forest products research because it adds to our understanding of the types and uses of plants in urban settings as well as the methods used to obtain them. Specifically the paper discusses the importance of plant use by immigrants living in urban areas of the United States.

Keywords: Cultural practices, ethnobotany, ethnoecology, ethnomedicine, human health, immigrants, medicinal plants, urban gathering.

5. Hurley, P.T.; Halfacre, A.C.; Levine, N.S.; Burke, M.K. 2008. Finding a "disappearing" nontimber forest resource: using grounded visualization to explore urbanization impacts on sweetgrass basketmaking in Greater Mount Pleasant, South Carolina. The Professional Geographer. 60(4): 1–23.

Examines how urbanization in formerly rural areas has affected gatherers of sweetgrass basketry materials on lands that had been treated as commons but over which private claims are now being exercised. The study took place in Mount Pleasant, South Carolina, and focuses on the gathering of sweetgrass (*Mulenbergia sericea*). Members of the Gullah community use these materials to make baskets, which command significant prices as a cultural art form. Hurley et al. used an approach known as grounded visualization in which grounded theory methods are combined with geographical information system methods to iteratively produce a series of maps representing harvesting sites and changes in those sites open to harvesters over time. Indepth interviews were conducted with 23 basket makers by using convenience and snowball sampling to select interviewees. Interview data were supplemented with participant observations of local government meetings and field tours with basket makers. Gatherers have lost access to many sites as a result of development. Additionally, the privatization of areas that were once de facto commons has cut gatherers off from areas where sweetgrass still grows. In some cases, gatherers can obtain access, but the terms are dictated by the landowners. On the positive side, some of the new developments are restoring native vegetation, and a few land managers are working with gatherers to ensure that they have access to basketry materials. The authors concluded that while sweetgrass resources and access to them are declining, sweetgrass continues to grow in interstitial spaces such as vacant lots and parking strips. These "fringe" ecologies persist in the face of urbanization, highlighting the shifting notions of property rights as development activities expand in rural areas. Importantly, some landowners have made efforts to both restore sweetgrass and allow access to those sites.

Keywords: Cultural practices, ecological knowledge, property regimes, urban gathering, urban political ecology.

6. Hurley, P.T.; Halfacre, A.C. 2010. Dodging alligators, rattlesnakes, and back-yard docks: a political ecology of sweetgrass basket-making and conservation in the South Carolina lowcountry, USA. GeoJournal. Published online March 24, 2010. DOI: 10.1007/s10708-009-9276-7.

Examines the role that amenity-driven urbanization plays in reshaping access to and use of nontimber forest products (NTFP) that are found on privately owned lands. The research focuses on the case of sweetgrass basket making, a key marker of the Gullah-Geechee culture that is historically grounded in ties to the land, and which persists in the greater Mount Pleasant area of the South Carolina Lowcoun-try. As rapid residential development has grown in the area, concerns about land-scape changes have led to a number of new efforts to protect the region's distinctive natural resources and cultural landscapes. These include efforts to discursively construct a regional greenbelt and "conservation developments." Yet, rarely do these discourses intersect in ways that resonate with the needs of basket makers. The findings emphasize the extent to which disparate conservation discourses—in this case variously focused on natural resources and cultural landscapes, but not local ecologies—remain disconnected from one another, thereby creating sites of NTFP resource conservation that are likely to remain inaccessible to basket makers.

Keywords: Cultural practices, environmental justice, urban gathering, urban planning, urban political ecology.

7. Jahnige, P. 2002. The hidden bounty of the urban forest. In: Jones, E.T.; McLain, R.J.; Weigand, J.F., eds. Nontimber forest products in the United States. Law-rence, KS: University of Kansas Press: 96–101.

In the late 1990s, Community Resources, a nonprofit organization, conducted a descriptive study of urban gathering for the Baltimore Long Term Ecological Research project. Researchers carried out semistructured interviews with 80 individuals, including environmental professionals, community leaders, vendors at farmers markets, and gatherers. They found that although few people earned income from gathering, far more people than they had expected gathered urban forest products. Gathering took place on public and private lands, in unmanaged to highly managed habitats, and from sites located in the inner city to woodlands on the city's edges. Most gatherers harvested for personal use, but many also gifted, shared, or traded products they gathered. Gathering was an important means for exercising social reciprocity and building social capacity. For example, holiday greens and seedlings were gathered and sold to raise funds for churches. Gatherers came from diverse socioeconomic and ethnic backgrounds. For some immigrant gatherers, gathering was a means to retain ties with their homeland, either through gathering itself or through the foods prepared from the products harvested. A few products (berries and chestnuts) attracted gatherers from outside the city, with some coming from as far away as New England. The researchers had expected that most gatherers would have rural roots, but instead found that many gatherers were urbanites seeking to build connections with urban nature.

Keywords: Cultural practices, immigrants, urban forestry, urban gathering.

8. Konijnendijk, C. 2008. The fruitful forest. In: Konijnendijk, C., ed. The forest and the city: the cultural landscape of urban woodland. New York: Springer: 49–62.

Konijnendijk examined the subsistence functions of European urban forests from the Middle Ages onward. Medieval cities had few trees inside their walls, but adjacent forests provided food, fuel, and fodder for the urban poor. Many of these forests were held as commons, and access to resources such as wood, pasture, resins, fruits, and nuts was regulated through customary rights. Others were royal woodlands or belonged to members of the aristocracy and were managed for timber or as habitat for game. Many of these wooded estates have since become municipal property and are now managed as public woodlands or parks. City forests in Europe were initially important as sources of wood, pasture, and other products. However, by the early 20th century, city forests became valued as places where urbanites could recreate and escape the stresses of city life. In the 20th century, European cities also began to view woodlands as important for water quality and nature protection. Urban forests in Europe have long been a source of food and fuel for city residents during wars and economic crises. However, the recent focus on recreation, watershed protection, and aesthetics in municipal forest management has led to a decline in the use of city forests as sources of products. Exceptions to this trend include Finnish cities, many of which still manage their forests for commercial timber production, as well as Paris' Forêt de Saint-Germain and several community forests in England. Additionally, berry and mushroom gathering are popular activities in many city forests in eastern and northern Europe.

Keywords: Policy, urban forestry, urban gathering, urban planning.

9. Nordahl, D. 2009. Public produce: the new urban agriculture. Washington, DC: Island Press. 236 p.

Nordahl described the diverse and expanding efforts of grassroots organizations and municipal governments in the United States to promote the use of public urban space for food production. These efforts include community gardens, edible landscaping, and public orchards, as well as fruit sharing and fruit mapping projects. He argued that municipal governments can simultaneously address food insecurity and environmental sustainability concerns by dedicating land and funding toward the production of "public produce." Such produce is public in two senses—it is grown on public land, and it is available for a broad spectrum of urban residents to harvest. Nordahl argued that urban-based food production systems will require thinking of urban trees and vegetation as providers of food as well as providers of ecosystem services and aesthetic values. He devoted an entire chapter to examples of efforts to strengthen and expand age-old activities such as gleaning and foraging in urban areas, focusing in particular on cities in California and Iowa. He contended that planners can maximize the access of homeless people to nutritious food by dedicating a significant percentage of public space, such as street strips and parks, to the production of edible plants.

Keywords: Community gardens, fruit sharing, gardening, gleaning, human health, public orchards, urban food production, urban gathering, urban planning.

10. Wehi, P.M.; Wehi, W.L. 2009. Traditional plant harvesting in contemporary fragmented and urban landscapes. Conservation Biology. 24(2): 594–604.

Examines the harvesting practice of Maori elders in Waikato, New Zealand, and considers the importance of various landscapes (conservation lands, fragmented and urban landscapes) as sites for traditional harvesting. The authors interviewed seven elders about culturally important plant species (for medicine, crafts and foods) and about where they harvest these species. The authors compared interview data with information collected on government permits for harvesting plants on conservation lands. Maori elders identified 58 culturally important plants that are currently harvested on a regular basis. Very few of these species are harvested from conservation lands; the majority of culturally important plant collecting by Maori elders occurs in urban public areas and along roadsides, and occasionally on indigenous resource areas. Findings indicate that urban harvesting reduces pressure on species that might otherwise be harvested in conservation areas. More significant, however, are the authors' findings that urban areas are vitally important for supporting the maintenance of cultural practices and identities of people in urban areas (particularly indigenous people who may have been dislocated from their traditional resources areas). These cultural values of urban ecosystems should be considered when managing public lands in urban areas. Moreover, the authors advocated for including indigenous users (and ostensibly, other nonindigenous harvesters with local ecological knowledge and cultural harvesting practices) in the planning processes for managing urban sites, arguing "the ecological stewardship approach increases the effectiveness of monitoring and assessment protocols and the conservation of urban biodiversity and has many other positive spinoffs" (p. 603). This paper acknowledges that urban ecosystems are important to gatherers and may even be more important than other nonurban areas. Also, urban public areas are significant for maintaining cultural practices. And finally, the paper positively links urban resource gatherers to ecosystem stewardship as an effective way to conserve urban biodiversity.

Keywords: Conservation, cultural practices, ecological knowledge, ethnoecology, stewardship, urban ecology.

Rural Gathering

The academic literature on contemporary rural gathering in countries of the global North provides many insights about gatherers and gathering practices that are potentially applicable in urban settings. We include annotations from a few key studies to highlight themes that researchers are likely to encounter in studies of urban gatherers. One common theme is that gathering is a complex set of practices and thus is challenging not only to study but also to regulate (Anderson 2000, Carroll et al. 2003, Emery et al. 2006, Love et al. 1998, Richards and Creasey 1996). A related theme is that the social heterogeneity of those who practice gathering makes the conceptual category, "gatherer" extremely problematic as it potentially includes people with little in common other than that they harvest plants or fungi (Robbins et al. 2008). As pointed out by Emery and Pierce (2005), efforts by policymakers to distinguish subsistence gathering from other types of gathering are equally problematic. Carroll et al. (2003) pointed to similar problems when policymakers seek to categorize huckleberry pickers into mutually exclusive categories such as "commercial," "subsistence," and "recreational."

Another theme running through rural gathering studies is that motivations for gathering differ widely, and gatherers frequently list multiple reasons when asked why they gather plants or fungi (Anderson et al. 2000, Carroll et al. 2003, Emery et al. 2006, Love et al. 1998). One of the most commonly listed reasons for gathering is that it provides health benefits such as reducing mental and emotional stress and providing opportunities for keeping physically fit (Anderson et al. 2000, Carroll et al. 2003, Emery et al. 2006, Love et al. 1998). Samson and Pretty's (2006) research on the Innu in northern Labrador indicates that diets rich in gathered foods may also be far more nutritional than those dominated by processed foods.

The rural gathering literature highlights the important role gathering plays in helping individuals and households maintain cultural identities and strengthen social ties (Anderson et al. 2000, Carroll et al. 2003, Richards and Creasey 1996). Gathering also provides opportunities for people to connect with nature. Long-term pickers often have substantial ecological knowledge, and many gatherers report that they engage in practices aimed at maintaining resource productivity over the long term (Love et al. 1998, Richards and Creasey 1996). Incorporating such knowledge into policy processes, however, is often challenging because of language and other cultural barriers (Love et al. 1998, McLain 2008, Richards and Creasey 1996).

Additionally, many policymaking processes are structured in ways that inadvertently exclude gatherers unless they belong to formal organizations such as amateur mycological societies (Love et al. 1998).

Rural gathering studies suggest that a variety of data collection methods, including participant observation, semistructured interviews, and regional and site-specific user surveys can be successfully applied to the study of urban gathering and gatherers. Multiyear ethnographic studies, such as those carried out by Love et al. (1998) and McLain (2008) are particularly useful for understanding complex socioecological interactions for specific areas or products as well as changes in harvesting patterns over time. Large-scale random sample surveys, such as those carried out by Robbins et al. (2008) provided less detail but are indispensable for gaining an understanding of the spatial extent and social distribution of gathering practices. Qualitative research conducted at a regional scale, such as Carroll et al.'s (2003) study of huckleberry pickers and Emery et al.'s (2006) research on nontimber forest product gatherers in northeastern Scotland and the Scottish Borders, is helpful for establishing broad patterns in the characteristics of gatherers, gathering practices, and the social meanings assigned to gathering activities. Finally, geographically limited user surveys, such as Anderson et al.'s (2000) study of fern gatherers and Richards and Creasey's (1998) study of matsutake mushroom gatherers are useful for managers wishing to gain a picture of resource users' motivations, gathering patterns, and social characteristics in a relatively short period.

11. Anderson, J.A.; Blahna, D.J.; Chavez, D.J. 2000. Fern gathering on the San Bernardino National Forest: cultural versus commercial values among Korean and Japanese participants. Society and Natural Resources. 13: 747–762.

Examines the noncommercial gathering of bracken fern (*Pteridium aquilinum* (L.) Kuhn var. *pseudocaudatum* (Clute) A. Heller) fiddleheads on the Arrowhead Ranger District (ARD) of the San Bernardino National Forest in southern California by people of Korean and Japanese ethnic backgrounds. The study examined picking experiences, motivations for picking, stewardship behavior, and sociodemographics such as age, occupation, and income. Data were gathered through a mail survey of 146 fern permit holders. Fern gathering was done primarily in family groups or with family and friends, and most harvesters had moderate incomes and post-high school educations. The two most common reasons people gave for what motivated them to gather ferns were to spend time with family and friends and to be outdoors. Other reasons people cited for fern gathering included to teach their children cultural traditions, because it reminded them of their homelands, and to have ingredients for holiday and nonholiday meals. Only one person picked ferns to earn money. The authors concluded that policies based on those for commercial uses are inappropriate for this fern gathering program. They noted that fern gathering on the ARD is "primarily a social and recreational activity that is laden with cultural meanings" (Anderson et al. 2000: 759) and which reinforces ethnic group affiliations.

Keywords: Cultural practices, gathering, identity, immigrants, policy.

12. **Carroll, M.S.; Blatner, K.A.; Cohn, P.J. 2003.** Somewhere between: social embeddedness and the spectrum of wild edible huckleberry harvest and use. Rural Sociology. 68(3): 319–342.

The researchers used a grounded theory approach to studying huckleberry harvesting in northeastern Washington and northern Idaho. Based on 93 indepth interviews of harvesters, they identified four sometimes overlapping categories of pickers: native harvesters, nonnative household harvesters, income supplementers, and full timers. In some cases, individuals changed categories over time depending on economics and life cycle. Differences and tensions exist among these categories along ethnic and racial lines as well as along lines of difference over picking behavior. The authors argued that the range of motivations for harvesting huckleberries can best be understood if one views huckleberry harvesting as embedded within a network of social and economic relations and activities. They asserted that labels such as commercial, recreational, and subsistence use are not particularly useful for things like huckleberries where people have a broad spectrum of reasons (held simultaneously) for picking and using them. They argued that part of what huckleberry picking is about is identity formation and linking of identities to the natural world. The tensions over huckleberries also reflect larger struggles linked to differences in views about the purpose of national forests.

Keywords: Cultural practices, gathering, identity, policy.

13. **Emery, M.; Martin, S.; Dyke, A. 2006.** Wild harvests from Scottish woodlands: social, cultural and economic values of contemporary nontimber forest products. Edinburgh, United Kingdom: Scotland Forestry Commission: 38 p.

This study looks at nontimber forest product (NTFP) gathering practices in the Scottish Borders and northeastern Highlands of Scotland. Data were gathered through 30 formal semistructured interviews with NTFP harvesters. Supplemental interviews were conducted via e-mail and telephone with another 12 harvesters. The respondents listed more than 200 products that they gathered, representing 173 species. These products fell into six functional use categories (edibles, beverages, crafts, garden materials, medicinals, and others), with edibles, beverages, and crafts being the most frequent uses. Most harvesters collected products for domestic consumption or to share with friends and family; none harvested large quantities for sale in the formal economy. Gatherers acquired knowledge about NTFPs through diverse sources including family members and friends, as well as books and field guides. Many gatherers mentioned that their gathering activities were an important means of enhancing their physical and emotional well-being. Key policy recommendations include the need to review current legislation impacting NTFP collection and including harvesters in woodland management decisions. They concluded that gathering remains an important activity for a substantial subset of the Scottish population and provides an array of benefits ranging from access to material products to enhanced social interaction to maintenance of cultural traditions and physical, emotional, and spiritual well-being.

Keywords: Cultural practices, gathering, human health, policy, well-being.

14. Emery, M.R.; Pierce, A.R. 2005. Interrupting the telos: locating subsistence in contemporary U.S. forests. Environment and Planning A. 37: 981–993.

Summarizes the major issues linked to policies regulating subsistence harvesting in the United States in the early 21st century. One challenge is that it is difficult to measure the importance of subsistence harvesting to households and individuals in formal economic terms. Additionally, there is considerable debate over how to define subsistence, and whether it is possible to make a meaningful distinction between subsistence and recreational gathering practices and between subsistence and small-scale trade and barter. The authors suggested that it is helpful to look at subsistence as being defined by particular types of relationships between individuals and between individuals and the resources they gather. They argued that subsistence gathering can be seen in part as the persistence of precapitalist forms of production relations, which are geared toward reproduction of social networks rather than economic profits. Emery and Pierce noted that the majority of the literature on subsistence practices in the United States examines subsistence rights guaranteed to tribes by treaties. However, they pointed out that subsistence gathering occurs in many other contexts as well and is likely practiced by people from many walks of life, ethnicities, and income levels.

Keywords: Cultural practices, gathering, policy, subsistence.

15. Love, T.; Jones, E.; Liegel, L. 1998. Valuing the temperate rain forest: wild mushrooming on the Olympic Peninsula Biosphere Reserve. Ambio Special Report. 9: 16–25.

Love et al. looked at who harvests chanterelles (*Cantharellus formosus* (*cibarius*) and *C. subalbides* (E. J. H. Corner)) on the Olympic Peninsula, as well as their reasons for harvesting and their harvesting practices. Methods used included participant observation, a mail survey, and informal and formal interviews. They found that harvesters represented a broad spectrum of ethnic backgrounds, social classes, age groups, and included both men and women. All of the pickers interviewed expressed the importance of being in the woods and the thrill of finding mushrooms as reasons for picking. Another value commonly expressed was the sense of independence and autonomy pickers got from harvesting mushrooms. As a rule, most were ambivalent or resistant to regulations. Many harvesters practiced stewardship behaviors and have acquired substantial ecological knowledge through their picking activities. Despite having similar values and norms about mushroom harvesting, considerable tension existed between recreational and commercial pickers. The authors attributed this to differences in ethnicity and social class, as well as the lack of shared gathering places. Authors suggested the need for forums that foster public dialogue on regulations so that commercial harvester knowledge and concerns are included in policymaking.

Keywords: Cultural practices, gathering, policy, stewardship, wild mushrooms.

16. McLain, R.J. 2008. Constructing a wild mushroom panopticon: the extension of nation state control over the forest understory in Oregon, USA. Economic Botany. 62(3): 343–355.

McLain draws on Foucault's theory of disciplinary power, which posits that modern state control is made possible through processes of categorization, monitoring, and tracking carried out within the framework of a panopticon surveillance system, to understand conflicts over wild mushrooms in Oregon in the late 1990s. A panopticon is a structure designed in such a way that a watcher is able to see all the individuals within the structure without being seen herself; the effect of the panopticon is to encourage self-regulation of behavior with maximum efficiency. Data were gathered between 1994 and 2000 by using participant observation, direct observation, semistructured qualitative interviews, permit analyses, and archival analyses. The U.S. Forest Service employees came to view wild mushroom pickers as destructive resource users during the early 1990s despite the lack of scientific evidence to support their beliefs. State and federal resource managers subsequently created systems for monitoring and tracking wild mushroom pickers. McLain argues that these systems remained largely ineffective until the Forest Service established a wild mushroom panopticon in the form of a centralized camp that enabled law enforcement officials to keep track of pickers and buyers with minimal effort. The article highlights the tensions and resistance to regulation that surrounded the initial selection and subsequent relocation of the camp, tensions that reflected deep differences in how mushroom pickers, Forest Service ecologists, and local environmentalists viewed humans' place in nature.

Keywords: Gathering, identity, policy, political ecology, wild mushrooms.

17. Richards, R.T.; Creasey, M. 1996. Ethnic diversity, resource values, and ecosystem management: matsutake mushroom harvesting in the Klamath bioregion.
Society and Natural Resources. 9: 359–374.

Richards and Creasey's study documented harvesting patterns, practices, and values
of wild mushroom pickers in the Pacific Northwest in the early 1990s. The impetus
for the research was the entry of several thousand southeast Asian harvesters into
the wild matsutake (*Tricholoma matsutake*, T. *nauseosum*) industry in the late
1980s and subsequent conflicts with the Karuk tribe, for whom matsutake was a traditional food. A variety of research methods were used, including a survey administered to 106 pickers of various ethnic groups, semistructured interviews with 15
Hmong households and 10 Karuk tribal members, and an analysis of matsutake
permit data. The study found that most non-Asian pickers were local rural residents,
whereas the majority of Asian pickers resided in northern and central Californian
cities and towns. Many Southeast Asian pickers stated that mushroom picking and
camping was a way to recapture the sense of village life back in their homelands.
The Karuk interviewees highlighted the importance of matsutake harvesting as a
means for bringing the family together, sharing resources, and reaffirming ancient
traditions. Many had harvested the same sites since childhood and reported that
they used practices such as spreading and replacing leaf litter from harvest sites,
aimed at maintaining site productivity. Richards and Creasey argued that current
Forest Service participation processes are ill-suited to encouraging participation
by southeast Asian pickers, many of whom speak little English, and reside in cities
located at a considerable distance from the sites where public meetings on forest
management are held.

Keywords: Gathering, immigrants, policy, stewardship, wild mushrooms.

18. Robbins, P.; Emery, M.; Rice, J.L. 2008. Gathering in Thoreau's backyard:
nontimber forest product harvesting as a practice. Area. 40(2): 265–277.

In 2004, Robbins et al. conducted a random sample telephone survey of residents of
four New England states (Massachusetts, Vermont, New Hampshire, and Maine).
Their study is one of the few studies that examine the prevalence of gathering as
a practice among the general population rather than looking at practices among
specific populations of harvesters. Data were gathered through a random sample
survey of 1,650 residents of Maine, Massachusetts, New Hampshire, and Vermont.
Respondents were asked if they had gathered from woodlands in the past 5 years
and if yes, whether they had gathered in the past 12 months. The survey showed that
roughly 26 percent of the respondents had gathered wild products in the past 5 years
and about 18 percent had gathered them in the previous 12 months. Robbins et al.

pointed out that this rate of participation is higher than many other outdoor activities, such as golfing, skiing, and mountain climbing. Gatherers tended to have more formal education, somewhat higher income, and were less likely to be members of racial or ethnic minorities than the population as a whole. Gatherers were also a heterogeneous group and included both wealthy and poor, White and non-Whites, and varying levels of education. Roughly 60 percent of the respondents gathered edibles and decoratives, 16 percent gathered cultural or religious products, and 8 percent gathered medicinal or dietary supplements. Virtually everyone harvested for their own use (88 percent), and less than 3 percent of the respondents sold the products they gathered. The authors concluded that wild plants "are normal parts of many people's lives" (p. 272) and that "the vast majority of gatherers are likely disassociated individuals coming from a wide range of socio-economic circumstances" (p. 272). They asserted that gathering as a practice muddies "the taken-for-granted divisions of public and private nature and society, which commonly dominate and define modern life" (p. 273), and argued that the study of gathering and gatherers has great potential to inform understandings of the diversity of ways in which people interact with nonhuman nature.

   Keywords: Cultural practices, gathering.

19. Samson, C.; Pretty, J. 2006. Environmental and health benefits of hunting lifestyles and diets for the Innu of Labrador. Food Policy. 31: 528–553.

Describes the deleterious effects on health and nutrition among the Innu in northern Labrador, Canada resulting from the shift in their lifestyle from nomadic hunting and gathering in rural areas to sedentary lives in towns and villages. Drawing on ethnographic data gathered over several decades together with nutritional analyses of wild and store-bought foods, the authors showed how the transition from wild to processed foods has resulted in diets that are significantly higher in fats and significantly lower in protein, vitamins, and essential minerals. The shift toward foods rich in fats and low in nutrients is most marked among younger Innu. Government policies favoring the delivery of health, education, and welfare services to centralized villages rather than to hunting and trapping outposts has contributed to a further decline in the percentage of the Innu diet coming from wild-harvested foods. Sedentarization and increased reliance on store-bought foods has been accompanied by a decline in physical activity among the Innu as well, with potentially negative impacts on both physical and mental health. The authors suggested four policy changes to address the health and nutritional problems linked to recent sedentarization of the Innu: establish a food policy that would encourage people to continue to hunt and gather foods in rural areas; reinstate the outpost program, which previously provided services to Innu living in hunting and trapping camps; promote ecotourism; and amend the school calendar so that children could accompany their parents on hunting and gathering expeditions.

Keywords: Food security, gathering, human health, nutrition.

Gathering Field Guides

Many field guides are available to foragers seeking to learn how to identify and locate the many plant and mushroom species of North America. Many of these helpful guides are full-length books, containing descriptions of anywhere from 20 to 500 species as well as accompanying illustrations. Although most of these guides have a North American focus (e.g., North American wild plants), some are focused on plant species found in specific states, such as Pennsylvania and New Jersey. With the exception of a few guides that give foragers specific advice on how to forage in urban environments (Curran and Taylor 1998, Gould 1991, Henderson 2000, Jacobson 2008, Page and Weaver 1975), most of these field guides do not include indepth discussion that covers this form of foraging. Rather, many include brief and to-the-point statements regarding safety precautions that foragers should take to avoid, for example, gathering plants and other materials contaminated by pollutants (e.g., auto exhaust), foraging in parks and other areas controlled by regulations prohibiting the collection of plants and other materials, and collecting poisonous or harmful species that may resemble edible species. Many of these field guides also contain nutritional information about various plant and mushroom species and include easy-to-follow recipes. Further, although foraging is clearly a practice that is encouraged by the authors of these field guides, many of them emphasized the importance of not taking "too much" (except for invasive species) and avoiding the disturbance of habitats. The span of time for publication of these guides indicates that gathering is not a recent activity in the United States, but a set of ongoing and evolving practices related to developing landscapes. Although few of these guides focus solely on urban or periurban environments, all of the field guides provide valuable tips and advice that can be put to use by foragers who seek species located in urban, periurban, and suburban settings.

20. Brill, S.; Dean, E. 1994. Identifying and harvesting edible and medicinal plants in wild (and not so wild) places. New York: HarperCollins. 336 p.

Documents over 500 of the most common and easy-to-prepare edible and medicinal wild plants found within the range of the continental United States (with the exception of subtropical Florida) and southern Canada. It includes helpful, indepth descriptions of wild edible and medicinal plants as well as over 260 illustrations portraying plant characteristics and plant parts as they appear throughout the seasons. The introductory section includes a brief overview of gathering wild plants, cautionary notes regarding poisonous plants, useful equipment for gathering, preparation methods, and an overview of nutritional and medicinal benefits of wild plants. In addition, this section touches on several issues pertaining to urban/periurban foraging practices and management. The authors warned foragers to wash any collected plants prior to preparing them and to refrain from collecting plants in areas that may have been sprayed with harmful herbicides or in areas near heavy traffic where lead pollution may pose a substantial health threat. The authors also advised foragers to never collect any rare or endangered or legally protected plants, thereby helping to promote their recovery and prevent their extinction. The majority of this book provides useful information for identifying wild plants and contains a species list arranged according to the seasonal availability of each plant. Each species description includes information concerning physical characteristics, historical facts, preparation and cooking instructions, nutritional content, edible and medicinal properties, look-alikes, and related species to each listed plant; some descriptions are longer than others, depending upon the author's personal experience with each species. This guide also includes a separate section providing detailed cooking instructions and recipes as well as an index for referencing various edible and medicinal plants.

Keywords: Edible plants, medicinal plants, recipes, stewardship, toxics.

21. Coon, N. 1969. Using wayside plants. New York: Hearthside Press. 284 p.

First printed in 1957, this field guide provides an overview of uses for plants that are commonly found along country roads, and features approximately 160 illustrations and 10 black and white photographs. The guide is divided into two sections: a section describing the various uses of wild plants, and a section describing some of the wild plants that can be found in these areas. The first section focuses on recipes, arts, and crafts that use wild plants (e.g., dyeing with roadside plants), medicinal remedies, and use of wild plants as decorations inside the home and as natural landscaping materials. There are about 90 recipes, and over 20 different craft ideas ranging from dolls and toys for children to making brooms and ink. The book also makes mention of about 30 dye plants and 60 plants with medicinal uses. The second section is divided into useful trees, useful shrubs, herbaceous plants, plants found in wet places, lichens and fungi, and poisonous plants. The book describes over 90 species of useful plants, collapsing some into broader categories instead of focusing on a single species, and points out another 37 as poisonous plants to be approached with caution or avoided. A reflection of its time, the book generally suggests collecting along back country roads and near highways and byways as they provide areas that have various amounts of sun and moisture allowing for greater plant diversity. Further, the author implied that collecting along old roadsides avoids the problem of wandering onto private property. The author also suggested that collecting along rights-of-way might also be a good idea, as long as the collector does not overly disturb the land. The author suggested people gather to provide themselves with free food and interesting conversation pieces. The book also features a chapter on bringing wayside plants into one's own backyard, which focuses on creating gardens in backyards rich with wild plants or involving the community and creating nature gardens on public and institutional lands. There is also a chapter on naturalist camping, featuring recipes and remedies that can be used while camping.

Keywords: Edible plants, medicinal plants, property regimes, recipes, subsistence.

22. Curran, D.G.; Taylor, B. 1998. Urban fruit guide to the publicly accessible fruit, nuts, and berries in Boston, Brookline, Cambridge, and Somerville. Boston, MA: EarthWorks Projects, Inc. 66 p.

Describes the publicly accessible fruit, nuts, and berries in Boston, Brookline, Cambridge, and Somerville, Massachusetts. Its focus is on foraging in urban areas. It includes information on a dozen species, organized within species by city, neighborhood, and street. The guide also discusses some issues related to history, liability, responsibility, and toxicity. It includes contact information for local open space organizations.

Keywords: Edible plants, toxics, urban gathering.

23. Duke, J.A. 1992. Handbook of edible weeds. Boca Raton, FL: CRC Press Inc. 246 p.

Focuses on edible weeds and includes a discussion about how eating these weeds can reduce the energy costs of producing and using herbicides to combat them. The introduction of the book focuses on how weeds can be useful, mentioning specifically a case of a weed being used to combat malaria. One hundred different plants are described; entries are listed in alphabetical order and include a detailed illustration and written description of each plant as well as a section that describes the plant's uses (both modern and historical) across various cultures. Distribution of the plants is described by using the USDA Plant Hardiness Zone Map, with notes on the specific states where the plants may appear. The author noted that these weeds are found nearly everywhere and mentioned gathering in urban vacant lots directly, but also expressed worry about the contaminants that plants growing in vacant lots and related areas may have. The book also has a very useful index of all the plants mentioned and their potential uses and medicinal properties.

Keywords: Edible plants, medicinal plants, toxics.

24. Elias, T.; Dykeman, P. 1982. Edible wild plants: a North American field
   guide to over 200 natural foods. New York: Sterling Publishing Co., Inc. 288 p.

Provides information concerning some of the most popular and common wild
edible plant species present in North America (excluding the subtropical areas of
southern Florida). Although this book does not include any indepth discussion of
the availability of various plant species to foragers in urban/periurban locations,
species that can be found in disturbed sites, such as vacant lots, roadsides, and
fencerows (e.g., places often found in urban areas), are mentioned. This field
guide describes approximately 220 plant species and includes range maps for
each species, noting whether the species is native to North America or introduced
from elsewhere. It provides valuable information pertaining to (1) identifying
plants according to certain physical characteristics; (2) the habitat types in which
plant species are found; (3) the uses of plants and specific plant components,
complete with helpful symbols identifying ways to use each species as food;
(4) detailed cooking instructions and recipes; (5) the seasonal availability of
each species; (6) references to closely related species that are also edible but not
described in the guide; and (7) poisonous plant species similar in appearance
to those listed in the guide. In addition, the introductory section contains clear
instructions on how to use the guide; background information surrounding
the uses, locations, and histories of various wild edible plant species; scientific
information on the chemical properties of poisonous plant species; harvesting and
preparation methods; nutritional information; and Native Americans' utilization
of wild edible plants. From an urban management perspective, the introduction
also considers "overharvesting" and the ecological damage that may result from
unsustainable use of plant species. The guide is primarily organized according
to the seasonal availability of listed species, with additional information noting
other times of the year when additional parts of the plants can be harvested and
used. Each species is accompanied by a paragraph-long description and color
photographs to aid foragers in locating and identifying them. There are nearly
400 photographs, and a separate section of the guide devoted to describing and
warning potential foragers about poisonous plant species. For reference, the index
includes both common and scientific names as well as an appendix with nutritional contents of selected species.

Keywords: Edible plants, nutrition, stewardship.

25. Fisher, D.W.; Bessette, A.E. 1992. Edible wild mushrooms of North America: a field-to-kitchen guide. Austin, TX: University of Texas Press. 264 p.

Features information on approximately 88 species of edible North American mushrooms and another 18 species that are poisonous and should be avoided, along with 180 color photographs. Each mushroom entry includes key identifying characteristics, its fruiting locations, a list of similar edible and nonedible species and how to distinguish between them, and a section describing either the species' edibility or its toxicity. Each section also has a full color photograph allowing for quicker identification. Authors discuss what a mushroom is, their taste and nutritional values, and a description of what tools to take while looking for mushrooms and where to start looking. Along with the descriptions of everything a budding mycophagist needs to know, the authors urge the gatherer to take caution around fringe habitats. Gathering near landfills and toxic dump sites is discouraged. Finding out which chemicals are used in areas such as lawns and golf courses is recommended before gathering, as is asking landowners for permission. The authors also suggested avoiding gathering along roadsides, giving specific recommendations about safety zones: 100 yards from interstates, 100 hundred feet from secondary highways, 50 feet from secondary roads, and 10 feet from one-lane dirt roads, also pointing out that vegetation and wind patterns will alter the safety zones. Power lines, railroads, firebreaks, and areas near industrial sites—areas noted for their use of herbicides or the risk of contaminated soils—are highlighted as being unsuitable for gathering. The book also explains how to correctly identify mushrooms featuring 10 illustrations showing the parts of the mushrooms and describing how to make spore prints. The introduction then ends with the "Mycophagist's Ten Commandments" which sum up the introductory information in a concise way. The book also features about 76 recipes.

Keywords: Nutrition, recipes, toxics, wild mushrooms.

26. Gould, D.R. 1991. Beyond blackberries: a foraging guide to the publicly accessible fruit and nut trees in Seattle. Seattle, WA: SockMonkey Productions. 46 p.

Describes the publicly accessible fruit and nut trees in Seattle. It focuses extensively on foraging in urban areas. It describes 11 major species available in Seattle, including identification characteristics, edibility, harvest times, and locations. It also describes the locations of fruit and nut trees in seven districts of Seattle. Other discussions include the legality of foraging, responsible gathering practices, edibility, and toxicity.

Keywords: Edible plants, regulations, toxics, urban gathering.

27. Henderson, R.K. 2000. The neighborhood forager: a guide for the wild food gourmet. White River Junction, VT: Chelsea Green Publishing Company. 240 p.

Focuses on wild plants in North America. It covers foraging in urban and suburban areas quite extensively and includes information on foraging topics such as tools and preservation. The book is divided into sections covering resinous herbs, broadleaf trees, flowers, hedges and ornamentals, greens, and roots. Each section describes several species and then provides recipes for their use. Photos, illustrations, and stories are provided for the species. Approximately 70 species are described. A calendar of seasonal availability is provided.

Keywords: Edible plants, recipes.

28. Jacobson, A.L. 2008. Wild plants of greater Seattle. Seattle, WA: Arthur Lee Jacobson. 496 p.

Focuses on wild plants in greater Seattle. It describes all types of plants, including medicinals, edibles, and others. It acknowledges that foraging for edibles is an important motivator for understanding wild plants and briefly mentions foraging ethics. It includes roughly 500 species and identifies them by their characteristics, scientific and common names, and provides additional information. Illustrations are also provided for many plants. The guide is organized by species and does not include locations for finding plants. History, habitats, uses, a calendar, and conservation suggestions are also included.

Keywords: Edible plants, medicinal plants, stewardship, urban gathering.

29. Kallas, J. 2010. Edible wild plants: wild foods from dirt to plate. Layton, UT: Gibbs Smith. 416 p.

With nearly 300 full color photos, this field guide introduces the practice of collecting edible wild plants, focusing on making collecting easy and accessible to everyone. The field guide focuses on 15 different but common species, which the author has selected based on the ease with which they are found and accessed. These species can be found in the reader's yard or neighborhood, an inducement for urban and suburban gathering. The author discussed finding these species in disturbed areas such as vacant lots. Species are divided into four categories based principally on taste considerations: foundation greens, tart greens, pungent greens, and bitter greens. Each plant has its own chapter, with full color photographs of every life stage as well as look-alikes (edible, toxic, and poisonous) intended to make identification easier. Distribution maps and lists of common names for each plant provide further information. The plant chapters feature detailed instructions on how to collect and prepare the plants, with recipes for every plant. The book also has extensive chapters geared toward understanding the concept of edible wild plants, how the author defines the words, and what people need if they want to get into collecting. Although the author does not mention any regulations surrounding collecting, he does provide a disclaimer that collecting and eating wild plants involves a certain amount of risk. Concluding chapters discuss the diverse reasons people may have for collecting as well as suggestions about the ways collecting wild edibles can improve social and family networks. Besides further encouraging individuals to create their own gardens of wild edibles, the book's appendices contain nutritional information and brief explanations about how these plants benefit people.

Keywords: Edible plants, nutrition, recipes.

30. Medve, R.; Medve, M. 1990. Edible wild plants of Pennsylvania and neighboring states. University Park, PA: Pennsylvania State University Press. 260 p.

Describes approximately 102 wild edible plant species found in Pennsylvania and other states in the mid-Atlantic region. Descriptions are well-organized, with each occupying two pages and containing identical categories of information. Species descriptions are arranged according to the size of each plant, moving from smallest to largest. Each species description provides common and scientific names; black and white illustrations; and information regarding taxonomic family, plant characteristics, habitat, distribution, the edible parts of plants, food uses, warnings of possible dangers that the plant may pose, preparation techniques, recipes, and additional interesting remarks, including historical medicinal uses of plants. The authors discuss reasons for foraging for wild edible plants; important safety rules to follow when foraging; and general instructions for how to go about foraging, where to find wild edible plants, and how to prepare and consume plants once harvested. The book discusses the possibility that plants may be contaminated from vehicle emissions and other harmful chemicals present in our environment and emphasizes gathering plants in locations likely to contain minimal pollution. Although this book contains no sections specifically focused on foraging in urban or periurban environments, it does discuss the possibility of foraging for wild edible plants in settings such as vacant lots and roadsides—which are sites found in greater abundance within urban areas than in rural areas. The authors also suggest that foragers obtain permission from property or landowners and learn about state and federal regulations associated with any potential foraging locations prior to gathering plants. This book also contains sections on the nutritional content of selected plant species, toxic look-alikes of listed plants, helpful indexes, and a glossary for reference.

Keywords: Edible plants, nutrition, property regimes, toxics.

31. Page, N.M.; Weaver, R.E.J. 1975. Wild plants in the city. New York: Quadrangle/The New York Times Book Company. 117 p.

Identifies nearly 80 wild plant species or suites of species that grow in Boston and other cities of the Northeastern United States. The list is not exhaustive but, rather, includes what the authors considered to be the most common, conspicuous, or interesting wild plants. A forward briefly describes urban successional processes and habitats such as vacant lots, roadsides, cracks in pavement, and water courses. An introduction discusses the ecological conditions and biological characteristics that allow some species to thrive in urban environments before musing on the role of wild plants and the city spaces that contain them. A majority of this 117-page book is dedicated to species descriptions, divided into four categories: (1) herbaceous flowering plants, (2) grasses and grasslike plants, (3) trees and shrubs, and (4) ferns. Each description provides information such as species height, leaf dimensions, habitat, place of origin, and growth habits, as well as one or more illustrations. Although not expressly meant to be a guide to urban gathering, many descriptions conclude with mention of uses for food, medicine, or dyes. Species descriptions are preceded by a key to aid in the identification of herbaceous flowering plants. The book is indexed and includes a brief bibliography.

Keywords: Edible plants, medicinal plants, urban gathering.

32. Russell, B. 2006. Field guide to wild mushrooms of Pennsylvania and the mid-Atlantic. University Park, PA: The Pennsylvania State University Press. 248 p.

Features 100 species of mushrooms, both edible and inedible, with color photographs at the end of each chapter. The mushrooms are divided according to the season in which they are available, and then further divided into gilled mushrooms, pored mushrooms, and mushrooms that are neither. Each gilled mushroom is presented according to the color of its spore print. The author gives a very brief overview of mushroom hunting and some advice to beginners, including a brief cautionary statement about collecting in contaminated areas and within 50 feet of roadways. Concise mushroom descriptions follow, with a few paragraphs devoted to where each species is found and a species history. Descriptions also detail caps, gills, the spore print, the stem, growth habit, edibility, any of the species' copycats, and other brief tips. The author includes four recipes that can be used with any of the collected mushrooms.

Keywords: Recipes, toxics, wild mushrooms.

33. Still, C. 1998. Botany and healing: medicinal plants of New Jersey and the region. New Brunswick, NJ: Rutgers University Press. 280 p.

Describes about 495 wild medicinal plant species found in New Jersey and surrounding areas, including southeastern Pennsylvania. The introductory section provides a brief account of the history of wild medicinal plant use, the author's personal experience with collecting such plants, and instructions for how to use the guide to identify and locate various species. This section also describes the physical and chemical properties of medicinal plants, methods of preparing these plants, harvesting directions, and cautionary notes. The guide consists primarily of a species list, organized according to taxonomic family and genus, and is accompanied by thorough descriptions and illustrations of listed species. Each description includes information on the average plant size, other physical characteristics; habitat, geographic range, seasonal availability, modern medicinal uses of plants, and ways in which Native Americans have historically used plants for medicinal purposes. There is minimal reference within this guide to foraging in urban or periurban locations, but the information contained in the guide can be applied to urban foraging. The guide contains a brief discussion of the current environmental problem associated with invasive species and the concurrent loss of native species in the mid-Atlantic and other regions of the United States. A set of appendixes arranged by medicinal plant use, glossary, and an index provide further reference materials for foragers.

Keywords: Cultural practices, medicinal plants.

34. Thayer, S. 2006. The forager's harvest: a guide to identifying, harvesting, and preparing edible wild plants. Ogema, WI: Forager's Harvest. 360 p.

Describes wild edible plant species in North America. Each of the 32 species descriptions contained in this guide draw on the author's foraging experience. The introduction contains an interesting discussion of general locations that offer good opportunities for collecting wild food within both rural and urban areas. The introduction also touches on the laws and regulations that pertain to certain foraging locations (e.g., public parks), including those that may prohibit the taking or use of plant species growing there; foragers are warned to be cautious when collecting plants in these areas. The introduction also addresses overharvesting and the importance of species conservation; foragers are cautioned to refrain from harvesting species in an unsustainable manner so as to ensure the continued health and abundance of valuable wild edible plant populations. Further described is the history of foraging and wild food literature, reasons for foraging for wild edible plants, cooking with wild edible plants, identifying plants and safety precautions, methods of harvest and preparation of wild edible plants, storage of these species, and ideal harvesting times and seasons for particular species. Each of the 32 individual descriptions that compose the bulk of this guide includes information relating to identification, the species range, habitat characteristics, seasonal availability, edible versus inedible parts of plants, harvesting methods, and preparation methods for that particular species. In addition, there are helpful indexes, a glossary, and species identification diagrams included in the back of the guide. This guide is organized according to taxonomic order of species; descriptions of related plants are situated side by side. This helps familiarize the reader with differentiating among plant species that share similar physical characteristics and will help foragers develop skills in identifying wild edible plants. The guide includes over 200 color photographs, which may also help foragers learn to identify edible plant species.

Keyword: Conservation, edible plants, recipes, regulations.

Popular Media

Articles appearing in the popular media reveal trends about urban nontimber forest products (NTFPs) that are only just beginning to be investigated in the peer-reviewed literature. They indicate the existence of both new and old gathering practices in urban areas, describe some of the tensions and conflicts associated with urban gathering, and discuss the environmental health risks associated with gathering in cities. Reflecting themes in the academic literature on rural gathering, these articles collectively suggest that urban gathering occurs in many U.S. cities, takes a variety of forms, and that motivations for participating in gathering are diverse.

Many recent articles highlight the emergence of organized fruit-gathering projects. These articles reflect the convergence of local food, food security (largely focused on low-income city dwellers), and environmental sustainability movement concerns. These articles speak to the diversity of these urban fruit gleaning efforts, as well as to the challenges associated with the coordination of activities that seek to link people who need fruit to people who have surplus fruit. Another topic that has received coverage is the emerging phenomenon of Web-based fruit-mapping projects that seek to increase access of citizens to public and privately owned fruit trees.

Both the gleaning and Web-based mapping projects are uncoordinated at a regional or national scale. Neither topic is examined in the peer-reviewed literature. Consequently, policy related to these diverse urban gathering practices, as well as individual gathering practices, is being created in a knowledge vacuum. To fill this vacuum, basic research about who gathers, what is gathered, and where gathering takes place is needed. Policy-oriented research examining the linkages between food security and urban gathering, the role of urban gathering in expanding access to locally produced food, and the role of social media and geospatial technologies in fruit mapping and urban gleaning projects is also called for.

35. Bleyer, J. 2006. Fort Tyron Park: where the fruits of autumn might include a summons. New York Times. 17 September 2006. http://www.nytimes. com/2006/09/17/nyregion/thecity/17ging.html?fta=y. (September 11, 2011).

Bleyer described gathering activities that take place in Fort Tryon Park in Upper Manhattan in the fall. Asian park visitors come to the park to harvest gingko nuts, Russians gather hawthorn berries, and other visitors collect jewelweed, pokeweed, mulberries, and linden berries. Although removing or mutilating plants is illegal and can lead to fines of up to $4,000, plant parts that fall to the ground, such as nuts and fruits, can legally be harvested. Park officials reported that they see gingko nut harvesters as providing a valuable service but discourage park visitors from cutting or removing plant parts.

Keywords: Immigrants, policy, urban gathering.

36. Gordon, D. 2008. Nonprofit groups reap forgotten fruit. The Star. 23 September 2008. http://www.thestar.com/article/503866. (September 11, 2011).

Describes Not Far From the Tree, a nonprofit founded in 2007 in Toronto, Canada and coordinated by Laura Reinsborough. The group uses volunteers to pick fruit and distribute it by bicycle and on foot. The program benefits owners, volunteers, and community groups that help the homeless and disadvantaged.

Related project Web site annotation: **Not Far From the Tree**. http://www. notfarfromthetree.org/. (September 11, 2011).

Keywords: Food security, fruit sharing, gleaning, urban food production, urban gathering, volunteers.

37. Green, M.E. 2008. Oakland's fruit doesn't fall far from the tree. San Francisco Chronicle. 30 August 2008. http://articles.sfgate.com/2008-08-30/home-and-garden/17123934_1_west-oakland-east-oakland-suzan-bateson. (September 11, 2011).

Describes Urban Youth Harvest, run by the nonprofit People United for a Better Life in Oakland. This program hired young adults and teenagers to harvest backyard fruit trees. Fruit donations were given to low-income senior centers and youth and community programs. The article also describes Cycles of Change, a local program in which youths transport harvested fruit by bike. Youths gain an alternate perspective on local harvesting through their participation in the program. The program is surveying residents throughout the city about food access and is creating a database of houses that have fruit trees.

Keywords: Food security, fruit sharing, gleaning, mapping, urban food production, urban gathering, volunteers.

38. Hong, H. 2007. City gardens: harvesting dinner and snacks from the grounds around you. Baltimore City Paper. 11 July 2007. http://www2.citypaper.com/eat/ story.asp?id=14760. (September 11, 2011).

Hong suggested that rather than going to farmers' markets for local fresh food, city residents should try harvesting plants along streets, in yards, and in parks in the city. He recounts memories from his childhood of Korean grandmothers, including his own, harvesting gingko nuts and acorns from trees along Baltimore's streets and in city parks. He describes his mother's delight in finding perilla plants shortly after immigrating to the United States from Korea, noting that "It is common in Korea but was an utterly unexpected and welcome sight in this strange new land." Other edible plants that he gathers in Baltimore's city parks include walnuts, burdock root, and wormseed.

Keywords: Immigrants, urban gathering.

39. Hsu, H. 2007. Roadside concoction: an expert forages for weeds, fruit, fungi, and other wild edibles. Dandelion greens anyone? Seattle Weekly. 8 August 2007. www.seattleweekly.com/2007-08-08/food/roadside-concoction-an-expert-forages-for-weeds-fruit-fungi-and-other-wild-edibles/. (September 11, 2011).

This article is primarily about Linda and Roger Urbaniak who live in Seattle, Washington, and hunt, fish, and gather about a third of the food they eat. Both have day jobs, but Linda also teaches classes on edible plants. Linda (age 66) has a mental map of all of the foraging hot spots throughout the city, including fruit trees on private property and city nature parks. The author also interviews Linda Conroy, a traditional herbalist, who describes the nutritional value of many wild foods, and how they can be eaten (e.g., in salads, pesto). The article mentions that Seattle Parks and Recreation forbids the removal of any plant or animal matter from its parks. The article cautions potential foragers about collecting foods within 10 feet of roads as the Department of Transportation commonly sprays herbicides on roadsides.

Keywords: Ecological knowledge, environmental health, regulations, urban gathering.

40. Kaufman, R. 2010. Urban foragers cropping up in U.S. National Geographic green guide. 3 September 2010. http://blogs.nationalgeographic.com/blogs/ thegreenguide/2010/09/urban-foragers-cropping-up-in.html. (September 11, 2011).

Features the emergence of urban foraging across cities in the United States. The author highlighted current research being conducted by collaborators at the Institute for Culture and Ecology and interviewed researcher Melissa Poe about preliminary findings of an ethnographic and institutional analysis of urban foraging in Seattle.

Preliminary findings of the Institute for Culture and Ecology's research highlighted in the article indicated that foraging as a practice is not new, and that more than 250 species of wild plants and fungi are gathered in Seattle. According to Poe, people who forage develop strong connections to the plants and ecosystems that yield important foraging products. In both the interview with Poe and the author's survey of other popular media coverage of urban foraging—namely, the New York Times blogger Ava Chin—Kaufman raised important questions about regulations, sustainability, and exposure to toxins.

Keywords: Regulations, sustainability, toxics, urban gathering.

41. Mahany, B. 2008. Foraging ahead in the urban jungle. Chicago Tribune. 8 June 2008. http://articles.chicagotribune.com/2008-06-08/features/0806040417_1_foraging-plants-tracks. (September 11, 2011).

This newspaper article is about Nance Klehm who lives primarily by foraging in Chicago. She has been foraging in Chicago for 19 years as a way to connect to the land and live a healthy life. Klehm notes how the taste of wild plants is completely different from store-bought food. She commonly meets first-generation immigrants, including Poles, Russians, Mexicans, Chinese, also foraging for wild weeds. When asked about eating foods that might be dangerous or toxic, she states there is more medicinal and food value in local food than in food brought into the city from other areas.

Keywords: Immigrants, toxics, urban gathering.

42. McGuire, V.C. 2007. Replacing neglect with peach trees. The New York Times. 2 September 2007. http://www.nytimes.com/2007/09/02/realestate/02nati.html. (September 11, 2011).

Describes the Philly Orchard Project in Philadelphia founded by Paul Glover. It is a nonprofit organization with the goal of planting fruit trees on Philadelphia's vacant lots, creating edible community centers. The project targets vacant lots in south Philadelphia and New Kensington, areas of the city where population decline has been the greatest. The goals of the project are to help existing neighborhood groups (particularly schools and community centers) plant gardens with help from interns and volunteers. The conversion of land into green space and gardens increases property values and decreases litter and vandalism. Philadelphia has started a new initiative, GreenPlan Philadelphia, and public orchards are part of that plan.

Related Web site annotation: **Philadelphia Orchard Project**. http://www.phillyorchards.org/. (March 20, 2010).

Keywords: Food security, fruit sharing, gleaning, public orchards, urban food production, urban gathering, volunteers.

43. Mulady, K. 2007. When it's harvest time, you offer the tree and volunteers pick the fruit. Seattle Post-Intelligencer. 19 August 2007. http://seattlepi.nwsource. com/local/328216_fruit19.html. (September 11, 2011).

Describes the Community Fruit Tree Harvest program operated by Solid Ground, a local nonprofit organization. The program relies on volunteers to pick fruit harvested in yards and along streets in Seattle's Ravenna neighborhood. The fruit is then delivered to local food banks and meal programs.

Related Web site annotation: **Community Fruit Tree Harvest**. http://www. solid-ground.org/programs/nutrition/fruittree/Pages/default.aspx. (September 11, 2011).

Keywords: Food security, fruit sharing, gleaning, urban food production, urban gathering, volunteers.

44. Nakao, A. 2005. Fruitful project helps the needy: homeowners also benefit from program that harvests backyard bounty. San Francisco Chronicle. 26 August 2005. http://articles.sfgate.com/2005-08-26/news/17385592_1_huge-harvests-grapefruit-backyard-fruit. (September 11, 2011).

Describes a backyard fruit gleaning program piloted by Village Harvest, a San Jose, California nonprofit founded in 2001. In 2005, Village Harvest had 200 volunteers and harvested 79,000 pounds of fruit from backyards and commercial property. The program emphasizes educational programs that teach people how to care for fruit trees. Fresh produce is given to food banks and a transitional home. The program is growing, but currently the only funding is provided by sales of jam made from bruised/unusable fruit.

Related project Web site annotation: **Village Harvest**. www.villageharvest.org. (September 11, 2011).

Keywords: Food security, fruit sharing, gleaning, urban food production, urban gathering, volunteers.

45. Pack, M.M. 2005. Harvesting history: an appreciation of the pecan. The Austin Chronicle. 5 November 2005. http://www.austinchronicle.com/gyrobase/Issue/ story?oid=oid:313554. (September 11, 2011).

Describes the history of the pecan (*Cary illinoinensis* (Wangenh.) K. Koch) in Texas and pecan harvesting and processing activities taking place in Austin, the state's capitol city. Archeological evidence indicates that humans have consumed pecans in Texas for at least 8,000 years, and pecans have a long history as a commodity. Texans first established pecan orchards in the 1880s, and the state now produces an average of 60 million pounds per year. Pecan trees are common in many of Austin's parks and yards, and many people harvest them for their own use. The city allows people to harvest nuts that have fallen from city-owned trees, but prohibits the shaking of trees to bring nuts to the ground. Many yards also have pecan trees and Pack described one harvester who collects more than 200 pounds of nuts from her yard every year. Since 1983, the city's Parks and Recreation Department has sponsored a program in which seniors volunteer to crack pecans for city residents. The program charges 25 cents a pound for processing the nuts and uses the money to supplement its funding from the city.

Keywords: Policy, urban gathering.

46. Priesnitz, W. 2007. A fruity harvest: growing community and creating a local, public food supply. Natural Life Magazine: 36–37. http://www.naturallifemagazine.com/0706/fruitharvest.htm. (September 11, 2011).

Priesnitz described a project known as Fallen Fruit, which is working to map fruit trees in public spaces in Los Angeles, California. Los Angeles law states that fruit is public property if it is located on a branch that overhangs onto public property. He also describes Common Vision, a fruit tree planting program that benefits inner city students. Common Vision runs a fruit-tree-grafting training program called Roots to Fruits and Harvest Hip Hop, a roots rhythm rap contest. Priesnitz linked these projects back to the guerilla gardening movement initiated in New York City in 1973.

Related project Web site annotation: **Fallen Fruit**. http://fallenfruit.org/. (September 11, 2011).

Keywords: Food security, fruit sharing, gleaning, mapping, urban food production, urban gathering, volunteers.

47. Rich, S. 2006. Mapping Tucson's fruit trees. Worldchanging. 25 November 2006. www.worldchanging.com/archives/005408.html. (September 11, 2011).

Describes Iskash**taa, a nonprofit organization founded in 2003 by Barbara Eiswerth with the goal of providing elderly and low-income residents of Tuscon, Arizona, greater access to fresh food. Initially the project focused on providing fruit to Somalian refugees living in Tuscon. Refugee students were recruited to participate in the Tucson Youth Mapping and Gleaning Project (http://tug.bara.arizona.edu/jpproject.htm), which included mapping fruit tree locations, harvesting fruit, and distributing produce that would have otherwise gone to waste. The organization now has over 70 volunteers and serves refugees from around the world.

Keywords: Food security, fruit sharing, gleaning, immigrants, mapping, urban food production, urban gathering, volunteers.

48. Seversen, K. 2009. Neighbor, can you spare a plum? New York Times. 10 June 2009. http://www.nytimes.com/2009/06/10/dining/10Fruit.html. (September 11, 2011).

Describes the urban fruit tree gathering movement across the country. It focuses on Asiya Wadud, who organized a neighborhood fruit exchange called Forage Oakland. It mentions the similarities between this exchange and others across the country, including those accessed through Web sites like neighborhoodfruit.com, veggietrader.com, and others in Oregon, Michigan, and Alaska. The article says that urban fruit gathering has two basic principles: fruit should not go to waste, and fruit is better when it is free. The article addresses issues of legality and pricing.

Related project Web site annotations: **Forage Oakland**. http://forageoakland. blogspot.com/. (September 11, 2011); **Neighborhood Fruit**. http://www.neighbor-hoodfruit.com/. (September 11, 2011).

Keywords: Food security, fruit sharing, gleaning, urban food production, urban gathering, volunteers.

Web Sites

Web sites are an important means by which urban gatherers connect with each other and share information. Web sites related to urban gathering fall into three sometimes overlapping groups: (1) sites focused on the mapping of locations of fruit trees, berries, and other nontimber forest products; (2) sites for gleaning or food-sharing projects that connect landowners having excess fruit or other tree products with people or organizations wanting fruit or other tree products; and (3) sites for projects that sponsor the planting of fruit and nut trees in public spaces. Blogs are also an important source of information on urban gathering. However, with the exception of sites with feral fruit maps, they were not included in this review owing to space limitations. Most Web sites related to urban gathering are local, usually to a city or town. These Web sites often address key issues related to urban gathering including property rights, monetary exchange (or free exchange), and public lands issues.

49. Appleseed Collective. http://www.appleseedcollective.org/. (September 11, 2011).

The Appleseed Collective seeks to increase the production and accessibility of locally and sustainably grown food within Guelph, Ontario. Their work includes mapping public and private fruit trees, sponsoring edible and medicinal plant walks, and harvesting fruit trees. Their Web-based maps are interactive, allowing site users to add fruit trees to the map.

Keywords: Fruit sharing, gleaning, mapping, sustainability, urban food production, urban gathering.

50. Champaign-Urbana Fruit Map. http://maps.google.com/maps/
ms?ie=UTF8&oe=UTF8&msa=0&msid=109653875096993106128.0004566f3d06
2304bcf61&ll=40.117430,-88.255234&spn=0.183539,0.291824&z=12&source=em
bed. (September 11, 2011).

This is a Google-based interactive map that shows locations for publicly accessible
edible plants and fungi in the Champaign-Urbana region of Illinois. It includes
apples, plums, cherries, mulberries, persimmons, bananas, serviceberry, aronia berries, crabapples, pears, chicken of the wood mushrooms, cattails, and filberts. The
map includes photos for some entries and information about fruiting periods and
possible contamination by pesticides. Some entries include cautions against picking
fruits on private land.

   Keywords: Edible plants, mapping, urban gathering.

51. City Fruit. http://city-fruit.appspot.com/display. (September 11, 2011).

This interactive fruit map is managed by City Fruit, a nonprofit group based in
Seattle, which provides assistance to residential tree owners interested in growing,
harvesting, and sharing fruit. They sponsor fruit tree harvests, donations, and tree
care workshops in addition to mapping fruit tree locations. City Fruit's fruit tree
map includes apple, cherry, pear, fig, and plum trees. Information about the precise
location, age, and fruit quality of the tree is included for some entries.

   Keywords: Food security, fruit sharing, gleaning, mapping, urban food production, urban gathering, volunteers.

52. Cleveland Fruit Share. http://www.localfoodcleveland.org/group/cleveland-
fruitshare. (September 11, 2011).

Cleveland Fruit Share is part of Local Food Cleveland, an online social network that
is working toward creating a locally based food economy. It relies on volunteers
who pick fruit in private yards, vacant lots, and on quasipublic lands. The volunteers share a portion of the harvest with the owner and keep the rest for themselves.

   Keywords: Fruit sharing, gleaning, urban gathering, volunteers.

53. Community Fruit Tree Harvest. http://www.solid-ground.org/programs/
nutrition/fruittree/Pages/default.aspx. (September 11, 2011).

This Web site, part of Solid Ground's Lettuce Link program, shares information
about harvesting from community fruit trees. It includes a comprehensive handbook on how to start volunteer-based fruit harvesting projects and describes actions
volunteers can take to help promote community fruit harvesting. Through these
programs, volunteers pick fruit from private yards and deliver it to food banks.

   Keywords: Food security, fruit sharing, gleaning, mapping, urban
gathering, volunteers.

54. Good Food 'N' Greenways Project. www.lifecyclesproject.ca/initiatives/ fruit_tree/gfgw_index.php. (September 11, 2011).

The Good Food 'N' Greenways Project is an effort to plant food-bearing trees in the public spaces of Victoria, British Columbia. The project is a partnership of Life-Cycles, five neighborhood groups, and the Tsartlip First Nation. Its goals include increasing community and regional biodiversity, mapping the community's green spaces, increasing the amount of fresh produce in the region, and raising awareness about the interdependence between the environment, food, quality of life, and public green spaces.

Keywords: Biodiversity, food security, mapping, urban gathering, volunteers.

55. Fallen Fruit. http://fallenfruit.org/. (September 11, 2011).

Fallen Fruit is a community-based mapping project that was initiated in the early 2000s. The project began with the idea of creating a map of "public fruit" in the Silver Lake neighborhood in Los Angeles, California. The group's founders wished to increase public awareness that fruit that grows on or hangs over onto public property is legally public property and can be gathered by anyone. The founders believe that fruit is a resource to be shared. Fallen Fruit has inspired fruit mapping efforts in other neighborhoods and in cities around the world. The founders would like to see fruit maps created for the entire United States. Included on the Web site are directions and tips on how to make an interactive digital map. The Fallen Fruit Project also hosts Public Fruit Jam sessions, workshops that teach people how to make jam from gathered fruit. The Fallen Fruit Project has recently redirected its mapping efforts toward active city planning that incorporates the planting of fruit trees in public places.

Keywords: Food security, mapping, property regimes, public orchards, urban gathering.

56. Forage Oakland. http://forageoakland.blogspot.com/. (September 11, 2011).

This blog documents and coordinates the activities of members of Forage Oakland, a group that maps and shares fruit harvested in neighborhoods in Oakland, California. It includes an extensive list of foraging projects in cities around the world.

Keywords: Food security, fruit sharing, gleaning, mapping, urban food production, urban gathering.

57. Fruit Tree Gleaning Project. www.nanaimofoodshare.ca/. (September 11, 2011).

A partnership initiative of the Nanaimo Community Gardens Society, Nanaimo Foodshare Society, and Nanaimo Community Kitchens Society, the Fruit Tree Gleaning Project links people who have extra fruit and vegetables with volunteers willing to pick them in Nanaimo, British Columbia. Gleaners are encouraged to share the food that they pick with family, friends, neighbors, or local food banks. The project also offers canning and dehydrating workshops.

Keywords: Food security, fruit sharing, gleaning, urban food production, urban gathering, volunteers.

58. Fruit Tree Planting Foundation. http://www.ftpf.org/. (September 11, 2011).

The Fruit Tree Planting Foundation (FTPT) is a nonprofit charity that plants fruit trees and edible plants to benefit needy populations and improve the surrounding air, soil, and water in villages and cities around the world. The foundation strategically plants orchards where the harvest will best serve the community, such as public schools, homeless shelters, drug rehabilitation centers, low-income areas, international hunger relief sites, and animal sanctuaries. The FTPF has programs in several U.S. cities, including Chicago (public orchard), San Diego and Santa Rosa (tree plantings at drug rehabilitation centers), and Hayward, California (edible school yards).

Keywords: Food security, public orchards, sustainability, urban food production.

59. London Orchard Project. http://thelondonorchardproject.org/. (September 11, 2011).

The London Orchard Project was established in 2009 by two permaculturalist designers interested in integrating fruit trees into London's community spaces. Its goal is to develop a "skilled community of Londoners to plant, care for and harvest fruit trees," activities which the founders see as important for "connecting urban communities and increasing access to fruit." The London Orchard Project focuses on restoring orchards, and offers courses open to the public on how to revitalize and maintain fruit trees. They also have produced Web-based maps of both historical and current orchards in and around the city of London.

Keywords: Food security, fruit sharing, gleaning, mapping, public orchards, stewardship, urban food production, urban gathering, volunteers.

60. Madison Fruits and Nuts. http://madisonfruitsandnuts.org/. (September 11, 2011).

This grassroots initiative is aimed at encouraging people to plant fruit and nut trees in public spaces in Madison, Wisconsin, as a means to expand the availability of fresh and local produce. Once the trees begin producing fruits and nuts, the produce would be freely available to the public. The project encountered considerable resistance from the city's Parks Commission, which expressed concerns about how the trees would be maintained and whether the park would be held liable if people were injured while caring for or harvesting from the trees. The project also maintains an interactive map of fruit and nut trees in Madison.

Keywords: Food security, mapping, policy, public orchards, urban food production, urban gathering.

61. Neighborhood Fruit. http://www.neighborhoodfruit.com/. (September 11, 2011).

This national Web site seeks to help people find and share fruit across the United States. Its current focus is making fruit consumption a more local activity. It creates formal, sometimes monetary relationships between those who have fruit and those who want fruit. They address issues of liability, payment, and labeling through their system. So far, over 10,000 trees have been registered. The project also includes maps of publically available fruit.

Keywords: Fruit sharing, mapping, urban gathering.

62. Not Far From the Tree. http://www.notfarfromthetree.org/. (September 11, 2011).

Not Far From the Tree is a fruit sharing program in Toronto, Canada that relies on volunteer harvesters. The fruit is split equally between the tree owner, the volunteers, and local community organizations. Not Far From the Tree is working with a local partner, Growing for Green, to develop a community orchard in one of Toronto's public parks.

Keywords: Fruit sharing, gleaning, public orchards, urban food production, urban gathering, volunteers.

63. Philadelphia Orchard Project. http://www.phillyorchards.org/. (September 11, 2011).

The Philadelphia Orchard Project plants orchards in the city of Philadelphia, Pennsylvania. The purpose of the orchards is to provide healthy food, green spaces, and community food security. Community organizations own, maintain, and harvest the orchards.

Keywords: Food security, fruit sharing, gleaning, public orchards, urban food production, urban gathering, volunteers.

64. Portland Fruit Tree Project. http://portlandfruit.org/. (September 11, 2011).

The Portland Fruit Tree Project began in 2006 with the goal of assisting fruit tree owners in Portland, Oregon, with the harvest of unwanted fruit, and redistributing the excess fruit to families in need. The project identifies fruit tree owners who are willing to register harvestable trees (usually on private property) and organizes volunteer groups to harvest these trees before the fruit falls. Volunteers are low-income individuals who are allowed to keep as much fruit as they want in return for their work. The remaining fruit is distributed to emergency food sites. The project also offers workshops on food preservation and tree care. The organization has plans to develop a community orchard program that would plant orchards in public areas in partnership with churches, schools, and community gardens.

Keywords: Food security, fruit sharing, gleaning, mapping, urban food production, urban gathering, volunteers.

65. Urban Edibles. http://urbanedibles.org/. (September 11, 2011).

Urban Edibles is a fluid network of Portland community members who share information about urban foods and foraging. The Urban Edibles Web site is a community-created database and mapping project where community members are invited to post the location (nearest street address) of a wide variety of available plant sources including nuts, berries, dandelions, and fruit trees. Each location or source is plotted on a digital map that specifies the type of plant and any additional information that might be useful for urban foragers such as accessibility, description of quantity, and even comments on taste. Also available at the Web site is information about lawful and ethical considerations when urban foraging. The group has partnered with other neighborhood projects to coordinate public education workshops, presentations, exhibitions, interpretive plant walks, and posters.

Keywords: Mapping, regulations, stewardship, urban gathering.

66. Urban Orchards-Earthworks. http://www.earthworksboston.org/urbanorchards. (September 11, 2011).

Earthworks' Urban Orchards project works to plant, maintain, and harvest fruit and nut trees, vines, and shrubs in urban areas. The project provides trees, mulch, fertilizer, and horticultural and organizing experience to communities interested in revitalizing. Earthworks monitors the new orchards for at least 3 years. Information about how to grow a community orchard is included on the Web site.

Keywords: Food security, fruit sharing, public orchards, urban food production, urban gathering, volunteers.

67. Vancouver Fruit Tree Project. http://www.vcn.bc.ca/fruit/about.html. (September 11, 2011).

The Vancouver Fruit Tree Project is a community-based, registered charity that works to increase access to fresh local fruit in communities throughout Vancouver, British Columbia. The group connects people who have fruit trees, people who can help harvest fruit, and community groups that distribute the fruit or use it in their programs.

Keywords: Food security, fruit sharing, gleaning, urban food production, urban gathering, volunteers.

68. Village Harvest. www.villageharvest.org. (September 11, 2011).

Village Harvest is a nonprofit, Web-based organization founded in 2001. It began in the Santa Clara Valley as a volunteer project of the local 4H Club and the Master Gardeners. The organization fosters community relationships, practices sustainable urban harvesting, and provides food to those in need. Groups of volunteers assist elderly fruit tree owners who can no longer pick the fruit that their trees produce. Village Harvest's 200 volunteers pick 80,000 pounds of fruit each year, mainly from private property. The fruit is distributed to food banks.

Keywords: Food security, fruit sharing, gleaning, urban food production, urban gathering, volunteers.

Academic Literature Relevant to Urban Gathering

This section includes annotations from the fields of cultural ecology, political ecology, environmental psychology, environmental health, urban forestry, urban ecology, and urban planning. Scholars in each of these fields have contributed to understandings of human-plant interactions. However, with the exception of cultural and political ecologists, rarely have scholars in these fields explicitly studied gatherers, gathering practices, toxicity of gathered materials, or the ecological impacts of gathering. Nonetheless, research in these fields can identify key questions for studies of urban gathering and provide theoretical concepts, frameworks, and methods of value to urban gathering scholars. Conversely, studies of urban gathering also can inform research in these academic fields. For example, research on the sociocultural values of urban nontimber forest products (NTFPs) would address a major gap in forest valuation studies, and studies of the impacts of gathering on urban forest ecologies could help land managers identify practices that support the restoration of threatened anthropogenic ecosystems such as Tokyo's satoyama forests.

Cultural Ecology

Cultural ecology examines the relationship between societies and their environments, and is predicated on the idea that humans are a part of ecological processes and structures. Whereas early research in the field focused on the way cultures adapted to changing environments, today cultural ecologists increasingly draw on actor-network theory to highlight environments as biocultural products of "complex networks of humans and non-humans" (Head 2007: 839). Recent work in cultural ecology focuses attention on the **positive** role of humans in ecosystems and the need for conservation policies that recognize that humans are potentially positive actors in the production and maintenance of sustainable landscapes (Head and Atchison 2009). Although most cultural ecologists study rural places and people, cultural ecology approaches are increasingly used to examine the complex interactions of humans and nonhumans in urban ecosystems. It is this body of literature that is most directly relevant to studies of urban gathering.

In particular, the subfield of human-plant geographies has much to offer in terms of methods and theoretical constructs for urban gathering research. Human-plant geographies highlight how everyday "nature" practices, such as lawn care and gardening, are bound up with personal and cultural identities, social class, and societal and individual views about nature (Head and Atchison 2009). This literature, which emphasizes the liminal, or "borderland" characteristics of gardens and yards, demonstrates the inadequacy of the binary categorizations (e.g., human/natural, urban/rural, public/private) that underlie much current urban planning and policy, including so-called best management practices, and points to the need for more complex understandings of how humans inhabit the world (Bhatti and Church 2001, Head and Muir 2006a, Longhurst 2006). Research on the cultural meanings and functions of yards and gardens also shows that caring for yards, gardening, and participating in ecological restoration provide important opportunities for urban residents to develop relationships with nature and to acquire and transmit ecological knowledge (Gross and Lane 2007; Head and Muir 2006a, 2006b). Importantly, human-plant geographies demonstrate that plants are an important medium through which humans create and maintain identities and social relationships (Longhurst 2006, Morgan and Poynting 2005). Everyday nature practices can have a huge influence on ecosystems at all scales, and because they are wrapped up in identities, norms, and values, they can be exceedingly difficult to change. The use of ethnographic methods, such as participant observation, photo elicitation, and semistructured interviews, have proved particularly effective for studying everyday human interactions with plants and for identifying the range of individual and cultural meanings, values, and norms associated with particular plants and types of landscapes.

With the exception of a small number of studies on urban ethnoecology similar to those annotated in the "Gathering Literature" section of this volume, cultural ecologists have been surprisingly silent about urban gathering. A logical starting point for research on urban gathering would be the development of studies that parallel the yard and garden studies described in the annotations. Integrating gathering into this research would expand our understanding of the range of human-plant interactions to include forms of interaction that predate gardening and yard care activities. Additionally, studies of gathering are likely to prove particularly useful in helping cultural ecologists break down conceptual binaries such as wild/cultivated, urban/rural, and native/exotic. Finally, it would be useful to examine whether and how the knowledge acquired by gatherers differs from that acquired through gardening and ecosystem restoration activities.

69. Bhatti, M.; Church, A. 2001. Cultivating natures: homes and gardens in late modernity. Sociology. 35: 365–383.

Bhatti and Church approached the debates concerning human-nature interactions through the lens of the domestic garden. They argued that everyday spaces such as gardens are important as sites where humans acquire knowledge of and form connections with nature. Additionally, they claimed that gardens reflect how people and society in general view nature and its relationship with culture. Bhatti and Church conducted a survey of 150 customers at three garden centers, including one in London, one in a periurban area, and one in a rural area. Respondents also completed a written questionnaire with open-ended questions at their homes. Many survey participants described their gardens as spaces that provided opportunities to sense plants, animals, and the landscape in multiple ways. Additionally, the study revealed that social interactions, past and present, are an important part of the meaning of gardens to many people. Bhatti and Church concluded that studies of home gardens can help us understand how "very personalized human relationships imbue and mediate human-nature relations" (Bhatti and Church 2001: 380), and thereby can contribute toward efforts to challenge the view that humans are separate from, rather than embedded in, nature.

Keywords: Cultural ecology, gardening, human-plant geographies, identity.

70. Gross, H.; Lane, N. 2007. Landscapes of the lifespan: exploring accounts of own gardens and gardening. Journal of Environmental Psychology. 27: 225–241.

Gross and Lane's study differs from most other garden studies in that it explores how meanings change for individuals over the course of their lifetime, rather than focusing only on present-day meanings. Gross and Lane used a grounded theory analysis, and carried out semistructured interviews with 18 people from 18 to 85 years of age in small villages and towns in the South Midlands area of the United Kingdom. For many participants, gardens offered a place to escape. However, what they were escaping from differed over the course of their lives. Respondents talked of gardens during their childhood as places where they could have a bit of space of their own to explore and play. Gardens declined in importance during early adulthood but emerged as important in later adulthood as spaces to escape from the worries and cares of their work and home lives. The opportunities gardens and gardening provided for active engagement with the natural environment was a critical aspect of this escape outlet. Ownership and identity became more important as people became adults and acquired their own homes. Among the elderly respondents, gardens became a source of anxiety as they became less able to care for them, and their relationships with their gardens became more passive. Gardens were also identified as places where people developed relationships with nature, such as with wild animals that came to their gardens. Finally, gardens also embodied memories of relationships with other people. Gross and Lane concluded that domestic gardens are valuable resources for maintaining psychological well-being and that urban developments should include opportunities for people to engage with gardens.

Keywords: Environmental psychology, gardening, human health, human-plant geographies, identity.

71. Head, L. 2007. Cultural ecology: the problematic human and the terms of engagement. Progress in Human Geography. 31(6): 837–846.

In this first of a series of progress reports on emerging trends in cultural ecology, Head examined how cultural ecologists are coming to (re)conceptualize the relationship between the cultural and the ecological. Head provided ample citations of recent work in cultural ecology to support her argument that the field of cultural ecology is undergoing a significant shift in how it approaches human-nature connections. She argued that cultural ecology no longer puts forth the view of humans as external to ecological systems, but rather envisions landscapes as "biocultural collaborative projects" (Head 2007: 840). This paradigm shift in cultural ecology has led to a more focused attention on understanding the range of environmental knowledges—technical, indigenous, and local—as well as the roles of everyday human practices in ecosystem sustainability. This shift has also created a space for seeing humans as "a force for environmental good as well as destruction" (Head 2007: 841). Head pointed to the work of European landscape ecologists as particularly influential in the shift toward seeing humans as important co-participants in protected ecosystems. She argued that similar trends have emerged in conservation biology, particularly within the field of urban ecology and restoration ecology. Head concluded that cultural ecology will be most effective if it continues to look for ways to meld the ecological and the cultural.

Keywords: Cultural ecology, ecological knowledge, human-plant geographies.

72. Head, L.; Atchison, J. 2009. Cultural ecology: emerging human-plant geographies. Progress in Human Geography. 33(2): 236–245.

This is the second of a series of progress reports on emerging trends in cultural ecology (see Head 2007 for the first report in the series). Head and Atchison outlined the contributions of cultural ecology to understandings of human-plant relationships. They noted that the recent flurry of relational geographies focuses largely on human-animal connections, and pays short shrift to human-plant relations. Head and Atchison divided human-plant geographies into the following schematic: studies that look at plants as food; studies that look at plants in gardens; studies that look at how plants are intertwined with feelings of belonging and the delineation of boundaries such as those drawn between human/nature, alien/invasive, public/ private, and urban/rural; and studies that demonstrate ongoing links between contemporary and historical human-plant relationships. They concluded that such work may permit us to "(re)imagine a future of diverse and necessarily sustainable human-plant relations in a world of ongoing change" (241). This article provides an extensive bibliography of materials that are relevant to understanding human-plant relationships, and as such provides very useful background for urban gathering research. Although an entire section is devoted to plants in gardens, gathering as a theoretical construct is not touched upon in this article, nor does any of the research cited look at contemporary gathering in urban environments.

Keywords: Cultural ecology, gardening, human-plant geographies.

73. Head, L.; Muir, P. 2006a. Suburban life and the boundaries of nature: resilience and rupture in Australian backyard gardens. Transactions of the Institute of
British Geographers. 31: 505–524.

Head and Muir explored the notion of liminal zones, which occur at conceptual and material boundaries when humans seek to place things, spaces, activities, and people into categories, such as nature-culture, public-private, or native-invasive. They argued that gardens are useful places to look at these boundary-making practices as these are spaces where the line separating humans from nature has often been drawn in Western thought. They studied 265 backyards and their owners or users in three cities in Australia by using targeted sampling to capture socioeconomic and ecological variability. They identified four categories of gardening behavior—people who had no gardens, people who planted only exotic plants, people who planted only native plants, and people who planted both native and exotic plants. They also found that boundaries between in and outside were blurred in most yards, with some respondents treating their yards as partly inside space and others treating the inside of their homes as partly outside space. In some yards, the boundaries between the yard and the adjoining nature reserves are physically blurred as well. The study indicated that people engage with nature in a variety of ways and confirmed that gardens are places where humans and nonhumans are actively made and remade. Because some practices and attitudes break down the human-nature divide, whereas others reenforce it, the authors concluded that ecologists wishing to encourage more native biogeography need to pay attention to the social fabric as well as the biological landscape. They noted that sprawl reduction policies reduced the possibilities for humans to engage with the environment in ways that create empathy for plants and animals, thus exacerbating the human-nature divide.

Keywords: Cultural ecology, ecological restoration, gardening, human-plant geographies, property regimes.

74. Head, L.; Muir, P. 2006b. Edges of connection: reconceptualising the human role in urban biogeography. Australian Geographer. 37(1): 87–101.

The authors used backyards in several Australian cities as a lens to understand the hybridities of suburbia. They interviewed people whose yards abutted nature reserves and asked them to describe their engagement with nature. These people were a subset of a larger sample of backyard owners interviewed for a broader study of suburban yard care behavior (see Head and Muir 2006a). Examples of nature engagement identified through this study included birdwatching, bird feeding, looking at the landscape, working the soil, and walking. They did not mention gathering plants. They found that interviewees differed substantially in how they talked about their engagement with nature. For example, the native species gardeners tended to talk about putting species back in, whereas the exotic species gardeners focused on the importance of making things nice so that the reserves could support many types of use. Restorationists had very detailed ecological knowledge based on observations they had made over time and often controlled weeds so as to encourage local species. Conventional gardeners were more interested in removing weeds as a means for enhancing the safety of the area and removing pests. The authors concluded that environmental managers need to acknowledge the complexity of human presence rather than assuming that it is a threat.

Keywords: Cultural ecology, ecological restoration, gardening, human-plant geographies.

75. Longhurst, R. 2006. Plots, plants, and paradoxes: contemporary domestic gardens in Aotearoa/New Zealand. Social and Cultural Geography. 7(4): 581–593.

Illustrates the ways in which gardens challenge efforts to divide the world into binary categories such as nature-culture, work-leisure, and public-private. Combining data from interviews of gardeners in New Zealand with the literature on the cultural meanings of gardens, Longhurst showed how studying gardens and their social meanings leads to better understandings of how nature permeates cities. Many of the people he interviewed saw gardens as a means for expressing individuality, but, at the same time, they often sought to conform to social expectations of what gardens were "supposed" to look like in their neighborhoods. Gardens were paradoxical in that they were simultaneously spaces of work and spaces of pleasure and leisure. Likewise, gardens troubled the private-public binary in that they were nominally private spaces but subject to broader social norms and laws. Gardens played an important role in connecting parents with their children and people with seeds, soils, and plants. They were also important as spaces where individuals could build self-identities and retain their links to cultural traditions.

Keywords: Cultural ecology, gardening, human-plant geographies, identity, property regimes.

76. Morgan, G.; Rocha, C.; Poynting, S. 2005. Grafting cultures: longing and belonging in immigrants' gardens and backyards in Fairfield. Journal of Intercultural Studies. 26(1-2): 93–105.

This article looks at how immigrants to Australia in the post World War Two period used gardens as a means for both retaining their ties with their homeland and forging new cultural identities in their new homes. Morgan looked at the backyards of 17 immigrants in a suburb of Sydney. He developed life histories by using open-ended semistructured interviews. Interviews were done onsite, and Morgan also toured and took photos of the gardens. The interviews focused on understanding the meanings of the plantings and practices of gardening relative to the interviewees' origins. Morgan found that many of the interviewees used their yards to grow foods that reminded them of home. The processing of food grown in gardens was often associated with larger community events, such as wine-making and tomato canning. Additionally, many of the backyards contained motifs of their owner's homeland, such as altars, sculptures, and temples. Gardens and yards also were places where these immigrants developed social ties to their neighbors, typically people coming from cultures other than their own. Consequently, the gardens and yards are spaces where immigrants combine elements of the old and new cultures. Morgan concluded that immigrants create new relationships to nature and culture through their interactions with plants in backyards and gardens.

Keywords: Cultural ecology, gardening, human-plant geographies, identity, immigrants, property regimes.

Political Ecology

Given that urban gathering takes place within a built environment characterized by complex patterns of land ownership and diverse management regimes, the interdisciplinary field of political ecology has a number of key contributions to offer research on urban gathering. A key feature of political ecological research is its emphasis on the role of power in shaping natural resource use and management, including the often unacknowledged assumptions about how resources are defined, and how resource access is determined, the logics and rules that construct what is accepted as appropriate use (Robbins and Sharp 2003), and the communities or groups that do or do not benefit from access to and use of these resources (see Hurley and Halfacre 2010 in the urban gathering section). Political ecologists have examined the intersection of changing property and management dynamics—community natural resource use and forms of enclosure (e.g., Hurley and Halfacre 2010), rural gentrification and environmental conflict (see Hurley et al. 2008 in the urban gathering section), the neoliberalization of conservation practices and environmental governance in urban and rural areas (e.g., Hurley and Halfacre 2010), and the production and management of lawnscapes as emerging commons characterized as moral economies (Robbins and Sharp 2003). This focus places social justice outcomes at the center of changing socioecological systems (e.g., Brownlow 2005, Heynen 2003, Hurley and Halfacre 2010). For example, Foster's (2005) research on community gardens in Toronto, Canada demonstrated the ways elites excluded marginalized groups from accessing plots. Another feature of political ecology is the examination of subsistence activities, such as gathering, and why these persist within the rural spaces of advanced capitalism (see Emery and Pierce 2005 in the Rural Gathering section). Political ecologists have also questioned the ways that elements of nonhuman nature become actors in the staging of human-environmental interactions and politics (Robbins and Sharp 2003, Staddon 2009).

Within the urban realm, the urban political ecology literature seeks to locate the role cities play as structural components of global economic and ecological processes (Keil 2003), examining the diverse ways in which nature in cities is transformed by capitalist processes and who does and does not benefit from this transformation. This focus has led to better understandings of the efforts by marginalized groups to resist ideological and hegemonic management discourses as well as the ways vegetated lands are understood by diverse groups within the city as different forms of nature (e.g., Byrne and Wolch 2009). In identifying the forces that shape the material, social, and discursive dimensions of urban nature, urban political ecology suggests two important directions for research on urban gathering practices. On the one hand, it asks how patterns of development and the distribution of urban nature potentially affect gatherers (Heynen 2003), what spaces are available to them (e.g., Byrne and Wolch 2009), and how they navigate power relationships with formal land managers and owners (e.g., Brownlow 2005). Further, it provides a broader framework for understanding how the production of green space can operate counter to gatherers' interests, and conversely how these processes benefit gatherers. In the first case, Whitehead's (2009) case study of the Black County Urban Forest in the United Kingdom suggested that injustices result from the management of seemingly banal species. In the second, Brownlow's (2005) case study of ecologies of fear in Philadelphia—while highlighting the role a demise of social control plays in maintaining safe parks—points to the potential of emergent weedy ecologies to produce gatherable species. On the other hand, although much urban political ecology takes for granted the centrality of capitalist modes of production in the formation of urban nature, gathering in some of its forms must be acknowledged as a noncapitalist practice (see Emery and Pierce 2005 in the rural gathering section). Urban political ecological explanations, in their focus on urban nature (re)production by noncapitalist processes and practices (Domene and Sauri 2006) thus offer us insight into the study of these dynamics.

77. Brownlow, A. 2005. An archaeology of fear and environmental change in Philadelphia. Geoforum. 37: 227–245.

Brownlow's study of Cobb Creek Park in Philadelphia illustrates the ways in which social control mechanisms influence the viability of socioecological relationships in urban areas. His analysis is based on a narrative analysis of data gathered through semistructured interviews with individuals and through focus group discussions with residents near Fairmount and Cobb Creek Park. Individuals and focus group participants included both adult men and women as well as teens. He found that prior to the surrounding area's racial integration in the 1950s, the park was viewed as a positive space within the community. Over the next 20 years, the park came to be seen as a place of danger and fear. This fear is reflected in the physical landscape itself, which Brownlow describes as a "weed based" ecology. Brownlow traces the decline in the park's ecology and its emergence as a landscape of fear to the city's efforts to get rid of black militants and break up the gangs that had come into the Cobb Creek community in the 1960s. Prior to the city's war on the gangs, the park had been seen as neutral ground and thus was a place where residents of the neighborhood could go to escape violence on the streets. In breaking up the gangs, the city created a power vacuum and opened the way for more violent gangs to move into the area in the 1980s. Additionally, the city removed the park benches, which meant that fewer people went to the park and thus the system of informal social control also disappeared. The result is that women and elderly have lost access to the park. Brownlow concluded that access to urban green space is linked to the presence of healthy and diverse social control networks, and that when such controls are absent, physical changes occur in the landscape that reflect the uneven distribution of power and work to exclude economically and politically marginal populations. He argued further that restoration ecologists need to understand how vegetation affects people's psychological well-being.

Keywords: Crime, environmental history, environmental justice, human health, parks, urban political ecology.

78. Byrne, J.; Wolch, J. 2009. Nature, race, and parks: past research and future directions for geographic research. Progress in Human Geography. 33(6): 743–765.

Byrne and Wolch reviewed the vast literature on urban park use and users and outlined a conceptual model for guiding future research on park use, users, and spaces. They pointed out that parks are important tools for promoting particular ideologies of nature-culture as well as mechanisms of social control. Urban planners and social reformers of the late 19th and early 20th century saw parks as important for promoting democracy as well as spaces where urban residents' could improve their physical and emotional well-being. However, in many U.S. cities, parks were also spaces of exclusion, with ethnically and racially specific behavioral codes. Leisure researchers attribute these differences to the limited physical mobility and wealth of certain groups, cultural preferences, and discrimination. Byrne and Wolch argued that these explanations pay insufficient attention to how park landscapes shape who uses them. They proposed a conceptual model for parks research that blends cultural landscape, environmental justice, and political ecology perspectives to develop spatialized understandings of ethno-racial differences in park use. The model has four components: the pool of potential park users, the nature of the park space, perceptions of parks, and the historical and cultural context of parks in general. Byrne and Wolch concluded that a blend of political ecology, environmental justice, and cultural landscape perspectives will enable geographers to better understand the ways in which structure and agency interact to produce particular spatial and societal distributions of environmental harms and benefits at local, neighborhood, and regional scales.

Keywords: Environmental justice, parks, research framework, urban political ecology.

79. Castree, N. 2001. Socializing nature: theory, practice, and politics. In: Castree, N.; Braun, B., eds. Social nature: theory, practice, and politics. Malden, MA: Blackwell Publishers, Inc: 1–21.

Introduces an anthology that critiques the ontological separation of nature and society in European thought since the late 1700s. Castree argued that "nature" is not self-evident and that views of what is natural are socially constructed. Much of critical geography centers on showing how knowledges of nature reflect social and power relations, as well as how these knowledges affect the physical world in which humans are embedded. By showing that these knowledges are social products serving specific ends, critical geography opens up the possibility of questioning those ends. Castree stresses, however, that one cannot separate the social from the natural, and that all material forms are more properly thought of as socionatures.

In other words, "...the physical characteristics of nature are contingent upon social practices, they are not fixed" (Castree 2001: 13). Nature is not merely socially constructed; it is produced through social processes and as such is inherently political. He concludes that anyone wishing to develop policy measures capable of addressing environmental issues will need to acknowledge the sociality of nature.

Keywords: Urban political ecology.

80. Domene, E.; Sauri, D. 2006. Urbanization and class-produced natures: vegetable gardens in the Barcelona Metropolitan Region. Geoforum. 38: 287–298.

Describes the tensions over urban vegetable gardening on public lands in Barcelona, Spain, a city where such gardens are typically not officially sanctioned. The researchers use urban political ecology as their analytical framework, a framework which they argued allows one to escape the nature/society dualism. They argued that the differing views of what kind of nature is appropriate for cities are largely class based. Methods used included surveying and mapping plots, direct observation, and interviews with 132 gardeners. Planners were also interviewed both before and after the Local Master Plan revisions that took place in the early 2000s. Domene and Sauri found that most of the gardens are located on the urban fringe, and are often sited on flood plains and slopes on both publicly and privately owned lands. Most of the gardeners were retired working-class men and had emigrated from rural parts of southern Spain. Gardeners cite multiple reasons for gardening, with exercise and fresh food being particularly important. Gardeners also view gardening as important for providing them a connection with nature, and many see it as a therapeutic activity. The authors considered the gardens to be examples of socionatures in that their production includes both material elements and cultural meanings. These meanings, however, are contested, with planners seeing the gardens as wastelands and inappropriate for cities, whereas the gardeners view them as sites of personal fulfillment and a means for retaining links with their rural identities.

Keywords: Environmental justice, gardening, urban food production, urban political ecology.

81. Foster, J. 2005. Restoration of the Don Valley brick works: Whose restoration? Whose space? Journal of Urban Design. 10(3): 331–351.

This history of planning article reports on exclusionary politics associated with efforts to restore a disused industrial site in the city of Toronto, Canada. After the Don Valley Brick Factory closed its doors in 1989, local residents began to discuss what was to be done with the site. Two opposing viewpoints were involved in the conflict. One sought ecological restoration of the site to encourage environmental education and ecological health; the opposing view criticized these efforts as the imposition of elite values on the urban landscape at the expense of the less fortunate. Foster concluded that this "elite" view exhibits a tendency toward social exclusion; a preference for ecological restoration; and promotion of a particular environmental aesthetic. She showed how the science and practice of ecological restoration have been mobilized in the pursuit of a politics of exclusion that empowers the elite to control the site's spatial arrangement and limit participation in site planning for those at the margins. This control by elites has limited access to marginal would-be users, allowing the site itself to become host to recreation activities (most notably, off-leash dog-walking) that in some ways undermine restoration efforts (killing of wildlife by dogs), but are a priority for wealthy visitors. Plans to use the site to enhance education and recreation by children have also been undermined by the prevalence of unleashed dogs. In sum, Foster effectively showed how power structures and environmental politics work to shape urban space, and how those spaces consequently reinforce the relationships that produced them.

Keywords: Ecological restoration, environmental justice, urban planning, urban political ecology.

82. Heynen, N.C. 2003. The scalar production of injustice within the urban forest. Antipode. 35(5): 980–998.

In this conceptual article, the author took a radical geography perspective to the unevenness of urban environments, and the political ecology of where trees are planted in cities and by whom. Urban forests have benefits and other spillover uses ("externalities") that include moderating the urban climate; energy and water conservation; carbon offsets; improving air quality; reducing flooding and rainfall runoff, and noise levels; providing habitat for wildlife; reducing stress; enhancing child development; and increasing the attractiveness of cities. Understanding the distribution of urban trees requires an understanding of planning policies, economic dynamics, and cultural processes. Heynen argued that the distribution of urban trees is often associated with income, with low-income residents at an environmental disadvantage. The author cited a study from Indianapolis comparing a map of median household income and urban forest canopy cover, showing a positive correlation. The author also explored the importance of scale when looking at who benefits from urban forests. For example, at a global scale, urban forests serve as critical biodiversity sinks, whereas at a micro scale (household), individual trees offer psychosocial benefits (e.g., stress reduction). Heynen explored the question of whether reforestation efforts should focus on an equal distribution of trees across all neighborhoods to mitigate inequities in income, or focus on larger tracts of land (forest islands), where ecological efficiency (e.g., improvements to wildlife habitat) could contribute to global sustainability.

Keywords: Ecological restoration, environmental justice, urban forestry, urban political ecology.

83. Keil, R. 2003. Urban political ecology. Urban Geography. 24: 723–738.

Keil offered a "progress report" on the field of urban political ecology (UPE) in which he sought to capture the tensions between notions of the city as natural and unnatural (in the sense that it is produced and maintained through human labor). Keil considered UPE to be derived in part from such radical, critical political traditions as eco-Marxism, eco-feminism, and eco-anarchism, and went to some lengths to draw clear connections among these roots and recent contributions to the field. The article then takes in turn each of the three concepts that make up the term "urban political ecology." Keil explained that the field tends to accept the urban as the "currently-relevant incarnation of historical capitalist forms." He cast UPE as a nebulous, but increasingly important subfield, addressing long-neglected questions in four "clusters" of research in UPE, including a body of work centered around Los Angeles, intent on rescuing human agency from a reductionist vision of urban development as a natural and inevitable process; another that focuses substantively on urban water, but more broadly works toward articulating a Marxist UPE; the third revolves around critical examination of urban environmental and economic policy; finally, the fourth takes an environmental justice approach to understanding environmental politics in the city. Taken together, Keil sees the nascent field of urban political ecology as a promising new development in understanding, and providing a critical political stance on, urban environmental questions.

Keywords: Research framework, urban political ecology.

84. Robbins, P.; Sharp, J.T. 2003. Producing and consuming chemicals: the moral economy of the American lawn. Economic Geography. 79(4): 425–451.

Examines the factors that push suburban U.S. households to use a variety of chemical products to produce monoculture lawns at a time when interest in being "green" is particularly high. Robbins and Sharp used a political ecology framework to examine the social, political, and economic processes that shape decisions about lawn care and to understand the ecological effects of those decisions at multiple spatial scales. Their study showed that the huge geographic area now under monoculture lawn cover is the product of the intersection of a sustained lawn care product marketing campaign to equate monoculture lawns with healthy environments, orderly communities, and happy families. They used a mixed-methods approach including an analysis of the lawn care industry, a national survey of 594 adults responsible for caring for their residence's lawn, and phone and in-person interviews with a sample of Ohio residents.

The industry analysis showed that demand for chemical lawn products grew during the 1990s, despite widespread evidence of the toxicity of the chemicals and other negative effects of monoculture lawns. Interestingly, use of lawn chemicals was highest among those who were most aware of their negative effects on water quality. Robbins and Sharp attributed this counter-intuitive result to two factors. At the macro level, lawn care product manufacturers have mounted an effective campaign to persuade householders that monoculture lawns are a sign that the owners have pride in their community and uphold traditional family values. At the same time, they also have marketed green lawns (produced through the application of chemicals) as places where yard owners and their families can connect with nature. At the micro level, the same values shape lawn managers' decisions about lawn care. People living in areas where lawn care chemicals were the norm felt an obligation to support their community by adhering to the same lawn care practices. Lawn managers saw traditional lawn management as a way to build and maintain family connections, and many stated that working in yards was important because it allowed them to connect with nature. Thus lawns have multiple meanings attached to them—they are status symbols, examples of collective consumption, a means to strengthen nuclear family ties, and a link to the natural world. Authors briefly mentioned the gathering of plants for food as an activity sometimes associated with lawns. They concluded that the lawn may not be a particularly special case of land use behavior mediated through the moral economy, noting that "sustained attention to urban ecologies may yet reveal the plural character of many urban spaces, from parks and gardens to sidewalks and houses" (p. 445).

Keywords: Human health, human-plant geographies, identity, political ecology, property regimes, yards.

85. **Staddon, C. 2009.** Towards a critical political ecology of human-forest interactions: collecting herbs and mushrooms in a Bulgarian locality. Transactions of the Institute of British Geographers. 34: 161–176.

Staddon's work examined mushroom and herb gathering in postsocialist Bulgaria by using a modified political ecology framework that puts humans and nonhumans on equal footing in the examination of the politics of nature. He argued that this framework allows for an understanding of the "phenomenal realities" that produce spaces and environments. Staddon understood mushroom and herb collecting not as a unidirectional relationship between gatherer and gathered, but as a complex network of interactions between collectors, mushrooms, plants, landscapes, birds, and a host of other nonhuman actors. Borrowing from Bruno Latour's Actor Network Theory, Staddon framed these actors as collectively constituting a network of interactions to produce the phenomenon of foraging. Drawing from ethnographic surveys of rural villagers collected annually for over a decade and a half, Staddon argued that, though forests provide for a diverse array of extractive economies (including timber cutting; gathering for food, fire, and medicine; fishing; and pasturing of livestock), the state has so far proved incapable of capturing this diversity in its "regulatory vision." Instead, mushroom gathering and other informal economic activities tend to upset preconceived notions of the proper use of forest resources. Staddon concluded that researchers and policymakers need to understand nature not merely as a backdrop in which human drama is played out, but as an actor in that drama as well. Staddon also urged us to acknowledge "alterities, aporia, [and] slippages"—those phenomena that arise unexpectedly from systems we think we understand, brought about by as yet unaccounted for actors and interests. Only by doing so can we approach a just political ecology.

Keywords: Gathering, policy, political ecology.

86. Whitehead, M. 2009. The wood for the trees: ordinary environmental injustice and the everyday right to nature. International Journal of Urban and Regional Research. 33(3): 662–681.

Whitehead developed a framework for an everyday environmental justice derived in part from the management strategy in the Black Country Urban Forest (BCUF), the largest urban forest project in the United Kingdom. The BCUF employs an understanding of environmental justice and urban space in which traditional themes of structural injustice are suspended and a notion of ordinary injustices takes hold. Whitehead argued that this notion of ordinary injustice is not simply a concentration of undesirable environmental ill effects, nor the immobility of the people who live near them. Instead, everyday spaces of injustice are produced when these two factors converge. Managers of the BCUF have sought to remedy environmental injustice by focusing on development of ordinary environments like vacant lots. Based on interviews with BCUF employees and managers, the case study explores how the BCUF worked toward everyday environmental justice through tree plantings and remediation of derelict sites with significant community input. Whitehead praised the BCUF's focus on "remaindered injustice" (structural inequalities expressed through left-over spatial and material landscapes), but laments the fact that its focus on ecological restoration has often served to hide "industrial ruination" behind "ecological screens." Furthermore, he is concerned that the initial interest and funds that enabled the BCUF project to operate are waning, and that the project has failed to empower local communities in any lasting way. Although Whitehead's final judgment of the BCUF forestry project is cautious, he provides a powerful framework for thinking about the challenges associated with access and control over the banal spaces of the urban environment, and the people who face these challenges in the everyday.

Keywords: Ecological restoration, environmental justice, urban planning, urban political ecology.

Environmental Psychology

The discipline of environmental psychology includes studies related to the restorative effects of nature on individuals and communities. Research in this area highlights the positive effects of both the mere presence of vegetation and active engagement with nature. Environmental psychologists also explore the impacts of active living, which encourages physical and mental well-being through environmental design. Althouhgh we did not find any environmental psychology studies that examined urban gathering, these studies elucidate many of the reasons that might explain the persistence of gathering in urban areas.

For example, studies by environmental psychologists show that merely seeing and being near vegetation in built environments improves emotional well-being (Fuller et al. 2007, Hull 1992), improves physiological health (Ulrich 1984), and heightens the ability of adults and children to sustain attention (Kaplan 1995, Wells 2000). Horticultural therapy research links direct long-term interaction with plants to improvements in individuals' physical and mental health (Söderback et al. 2004). Stress reduction and heightened feelings of connectedness with the biophysical world figure high on the list of benefits individuals derive from their participation in urban restoration ecology projects (Miles et al. 1998) and gardening (Kaplan 1973). Additionally, activities such as gardening, tree planting, and ecological restoration can affect positively both social relationships within neighborhoods and strengthen connections between older and younger generations (see Westphal 2003 and Kuo 2003 in the urban forestry section). These diverse positive feedbacks associated with human interactions with plants can reasonably be hypothesized to extend to urban nontimber forest product gathering. Indeed, gatherers interviewed in many of the studies included in the gathering section of this document indicate that mood improvement and stress reduction are key reasons why they practice gathering. Studies that explore whether and how participation in urban gathering activities affects stress, mood, and cognitive function in both adults and children would be a significant new contribution to the field of environmental psychology.

Environmental psychologists also have shown that the presence of vegetation may result in reduced crime in public housing sites (Kuo and Sullivan 2001). Donovan and Prestemon's (2010) study of crime and vegetation for single-family homes in Portland, Oregon, showed that crime occurrences were consistently lower in areas with street trees. A caveat to these studies is that under some circumstances, the presence of vegetation—particularly vegetation perceived as overgrown or that obstructs views—can produce negative reactions and feelings of insecurity (Brownlow 2005, Talbot and Kaplan 1984). Such fears may be justified as Donovan and Prestemon (2010) found that crime occurrences in their study site were higher in single-family residential areas dominated by smaller trees that obstructed first-floor window views.

In their work on human psychological responses to landscapes, Nassauer (1995) and Nassauer et al. (2010) reported that well-manicured vegetated landscapes tend to be viewed more favorably than "messy" landscapes. However, they pointed out that this poses a problem for ecological restoration programs as the goals of such programs often are to produce landscapes many people perceive of as overgrown and disorderly. Linking these studies to gathering in a practical fashion, urban planners might wish to encourage gathering in some types of green spaces to foster a more manicured look while maintaining the structures and functions of restored ecosystems. A potential side benefit is that the presence of gatherers on a regular basis might serve as an informal surveillance network that could increase park users' feelings of security.

87. Donovan, G.H.; Prestemon, J.P. 2010. The effect of trees on crime in Portland, Oregon. Environment and Behavior. Online version published October 19, 2010. DOI: 10.1177/0013916510383238.

Examines the relationships between vegetation and crime occurrences in single-family residential areas controlling for differences in vegetation structure. Donovan and Prestemon used Routine Activity theory as a guide for understanding the effects of trees on crimes. Adapting this theory to trees, they postulated that trees could affect crime by obstructing views, thereby reducing the risk to criminals of getting caught while also reducing the effectiveness of surveillance systems. Trees might also attract people to public spaces, however, which would increase the risk to criminals of being seen. They used tree size and location to assess the degree to which trees obstructed views. The study was conducted in one police precinct in Portland, Oregon, with a sample size of 2,813 single-family homes. County crime data for the precinct was analyzed by using a geographic information system to determine the number of crimes within 50, 100, and 200 m of each house. In addition to measuring the number and size of trees around each building, other factors, including type of building, porches, fences, window bars, and streetlights were incorporated into the model. Donovan and Prestemon found that the presence of trees had a mixed effect on crime occurrences. Smaller trees that blocked views from first-story windows were positively associated with crime occurrences, whereas larger trees and street trees were negatively associated with crime occurrences. The authors provided two possible explanations for their findings. One explanation is that the presence of larger trees is a sign of a well-maintained neighborhood and thus criminal behavior is more likely to be noticed. The other explanation is that trees in public spaces (i.e., street trees) attract passers-by and thus discourage criminals.

Keywords: Crime, environmental psychology, urban forestry.

88. Fuller, R.A.; Irvine, K.N.; Devine-Wright, P.; Warren, P.H.; Gaston, K.J. 2007. Psychological benefits of greenspace increase with biodiversity. Biology Letters. 3(4): 390–394.

Fuller et al. examined how species richness in urban green spaces is related to psychological well-being. The study was conducted in Sheffield, United Kingdom, in 2005. Species richness was calculated for plants, butterflies, and birds. The researchers surveyed 312 green space users to measure how being in or near green spaces affected respondents mental fatigue, emotional attachment to green space, and sense of identity. They also asked respondents to provide an assessment of species richness for the green spaces included in the study. The study lends support to the hypothesis that species richness and green space user well-being are positively linked. However, they found that respondents were better able to assess plant species richness than bird or butterfly species richness. They concluded that heterogeneity in structure, as well as species diversity, may be an important element of psychological well-being associated with green spaces. An important implication of this research for policymakers is that consideration must be given to both the quality and quantity of green spaces available to urban residents.

Keywords: Biodiversity, ecological knowledge, environmental psychology, green space, human health, urban ecology, well-being.

89. Hull, R.B.I. 1992. Brief encounters with urban forests produce moods that matter. Journal of Arboriculture. 18(6): 322–324.

Hull surveyed 108 people visiting a community park in 1992, asking them to describe their mood based on Thayer's Mood Activation Checklist (energetic, tired, calm, anxious). The location of the park is not indicated in the article. He interviewed park visitors as they were entering the park and then as they were leaving the park. He asked those leaving the park to list up to 3 activities from a list of 12 developed by Hull that they had done while at the park as a way to rate the activeness or passiveness of their visit. Gathering was not included on Hull's list. Improvements in mood most commonly took place within 30 minutes of entering the park. More active visitors had higher increases in mood changes, but the link was not very strong. Hull concluded that visiting urban parks is associated with positive moods. The study also showed that the effect tends to occur fairly quickly. He speculated that just having views of nature should improve people's moods and argued that planners should integrate more trees into roadsides, schools, prisons, streets, and residential communities.

Keywords: Environmental psychology, human health, urban forestry, urban planning.

90. Kaplan, R. 1973. Some psychological benefits of gardening. Environment and Behavior. 5(2): 145–162.

Carried out in 1971, Kaplan's now-classic study of the benefits that people derive from gardening helped lay the groundwork for legitimizing studies of "everyday" nature within the discipline of environmental psychology. Survey questionnaires were administered to a nonrandom sample of three types of gardeners: 29 participants in a community-based garden operated as a communal endeavor, 50 individuals with garden plots at their homes, and 17 people with access to individual plots in community-based gardens. The location of the study is not indicated. Home gardeners expressed much higher levels of satisfaction with their gardening than either of the other two groups. Vegetable growers were more likely to emphasize tangible outcomes such as producing food or cutting food expenses as a benefit of gardening. Flower growers were more likely to list nontangibles such as relaxation, pleasure, and having a sense of accomplishment as the benefits of gardening. No differences were found along gender, age, education level, or experience with respect to the benefits of gardening. Kaplan concluded that "gardening plays a role in people's lives not unlike that played by more dramatic, more distant and less frequent encounters with nature" (Kaplan 1973: 159). She argued that the appeal of gardening lies in the opportunities it provides for humans to meet deeply ingrained information processing needs while engaging with natural processes and objects.

Keywords: Environmental psychology, gardening, human health.

91. Kaplan, S. 1995. The restorative benefits of nature: toward an integrative framework. Journal of Environmental Psychology. 15: 169–182.

Identifies the restorative power of natural environments to alleviate fatigue. Kaplan outlined a conceptual framework that explains how being in natural environments helps alleviate fatigue and reduce stress. The key to the framework is an attentional mechanism Kaplan labels "directed attention." This mechanism requires effort, can be controlled, and is susceptible to fatigue. He argued that directed attention fatigue is a key factor leading to ineffectiveness and stress, and that activities that induce fascination can provide relief. Kaplan uses the term fascination to refer to activities that are intrinsically compelling and thereby require effortless attention.

However, fascination alone is insufficient to relieve directed attention fatigue. Other components of the framework include being in an environment that shifts one's perspective (being away), is rich yet coherent (extent), and where one can engage in activities without struggling (compatibility). Kaplan noted that many activities that occur in natural settings such as hunting, fishing, gardening, and bird watching have all four components. He argued further that directed attention is a resource, and that the depletion of this resource, or attentional fatigue, is the cause of stress. He concluded that taking part in activities in natural landscapes restores attention resources and thereby has the ability to decrease and prevent stress.

Keywords: Environmental psychology, human health.

92. Kuo, F.E.; Sullivan, W.C. 2001. Environment and crime in the inner city: Does vegetation reduce crime? Environment and Behavior. 33(3): 346–367.

Examines the belief that vegetation conceals and facilitates malicious acts. The authors gathered police reports on crimes committed in and around 98 apartment buildings in an inner city neighborhood in Chicago and then looked at whether the vegetation density around the buildings could be used to predict crime. By using a series of regression analyses, the authors found a negative relationship between vegetation density and crimes, even when the data were controlled for potentially confounding factors such as number of residents, vacancy rates, and building height. This relationship held true for both violent and property crimes. They conclude that high-canopy trees and other visibility-preserving forms of vegetation such as grassy areas do not promote crime and may actually deter crime by increasing surveillance and by mitigating mental fatigue.

Keywords: Crime, environmental psychology.

93. Miles, I.; Sullivan, W.C.; Kuo, F.E. 1998. Ecological restoration volunteers: the benefits of participation. Urban Ecosystems. 2: 27–41.
Systematically measures the benefits volunteers derive from participating in ecosystem restoration activities. A random selection of participants in the Chicago metropolitan area's Volunteer Stewardship Network was asked to complete a survey with questions designed to measure levels of satisfaction with both restoration activities and life in general, as well as level of involvement in restoration activities. A total of 306 people completed the survey. Ratings were high for all categories of satisfaction, suggesting that restoration volunteering provides a multifaceted and highly meaningful experience for most participants. However, volunteers with higher levels of involvement and more responsibility had higher satisfaction levels. The study suggests that like gardening, restoration work provides participants

with a challenging, yet rewarding, opportunity to interact with nature, and results in enhanced feelings of personal well-being. These feelings are enhanced by the satisfactions associated with doing volunteer work. The study demonstrates that other forms of "nature-work" have psychological benefits similar to those associated with gardening. The study is important for urban gathering because it suggests the strong possibility that gathering would provide similar types of psychological benefits.

Keywords: Ecological restoration, environmental psychology, volunteers.

94. Nassauer, J.I. 1995. Messy ecosystems, orderly frames. Landscape Journal. 14(2): 161–170.

In this essay on landscape design, Nassauer argued that humans interpret landscapes through cultural lenses and concluded that when evaluating ecological quality, "What is good may not look good, and what looks good may not be good" (p. 161). She pointed out that resistance to landscape restoration programs is often rooted in cultural perceptions of what landscapes ought to look like, and the dominant view is that tidy landscapes reflect civic pride, neighborliness, and individual worth. Yet, such tidy landscapes often impede ecological functions. Nassauer also highlighted the difficulties of distinguishing visually between "natural" and anthropogenic landscapes. Although research on landscape perceptions clearly shows that most people prefer "natural" looking landscapes, what people consider "natural" looking is influenced by their cultural background. Nassauer described the results of a study in a Midwestern suburb in which respondents were asked to rate images of different home landscapes. She found that neat and well cared for landscapes were identified as the most attractive, whereas the most ecologically complex designs were considered least attractive. She argued that landscape designers need to use "cues to care" when designing more biodiverse landscapes. Cues to care are landscape elements that make it clear that messy landscapes are part of an intended pattern. These cues are culturally specific and might include such things as mowing in some areas (but not in others), wildlife feeders, and trimmed shrubs. She cited an example of a wetland project that used large bands of wet meadow plants as cues to care to give an orderly appearance to the restored wetland in its initial phases. She concluded that the use of orderly frames for otherwise messy landscapes can enhance acceptance of new landscape patterns.

Keywords: Urban ecology, urban planning, vegetation preferences.

95. Nassauer, J.I.; Wang, Z.; Dayrell, E. 2010. What will the neighbors think? Cultural norms and ecological design. Landscape and Urban Planning. 92: 282–292.

Nassauer et al. described how cultural norms influence ecological design adoption in periurban residential areas. They argued that city landscapes have an inherently public quality to them as they can be seen by anyone and thus are subject to being judged. They noted that certain "cues to care," such as mown lawns, dominate American conceptions of what yards ought to look like. These conventions pose a challenge to ecological design projects that emphasize less orderly landscapes. Nassauer et al. looked at how the appearance of neighboring yards affected homeowner perceptions of how attractive their yards were. They conducted a Web survey of 494 homeowners in southeast Michigan and asked respondents to choose among five different front yard landscape design alternatives. They found that most respondents preferred the conventional yard design and also that their preferences tended to follow neighborhood norms. When cultural norms and neighborhood norms conflicted, however, the neighborhood norms dominated. The authors concluded that new ecological designs are likely to be more successful if introduced at the scale of neighborhoods rather than individual properties.

Keywords: Cultural practices, urban planning, vegetation preferences, yards.

96. Söderback, I.; Söderström, M.; Schälander, E. 2004. Horticultural therapy: the healing garden and gardening in rehabilitation measures at Danderyd Hospital Rehabilitation Clinic, Sweden. Pediatric Rehabilitation. 7(4): 245–260.

Söderback et al. briefly reviewed the history of horticulture therapy in Western Europe during the 20th century, and then described Sweden's Danderyd Hospital Horticultural Therapy Garden and its associated horticultural therapy program. Healing gardens and gardening first gained importance in hospital settings as treatments for mental health patients. Over time, hospitals developed a diverse set of horticultural treatments, including active gardening, making gardens available for patients to sit in, and incorporating plants into hospital interior design. They also expanded these techniques to treat clients with physical and developmental disabilities, as well as mental health clients. Söderback et al. provided sketches of the physical layout of the Danderyd Horticultural Therapy Garden to illustrate how elements of a built landscape can be structured to address multiple sensory, emotional, and healing needs. Of particular interest for urban gathering researchers is the list of specific plant species associated with different therapeutic uses.

Keywords: Environmental psychology, gardening, human health.

97. Talbot, J.F.; Kaplan, R. 1984. Needs and fears: the response to trees and nature in the inner city. Journal of Arboriculture. 10(8): 222–228.

Examines preferences of 97 Black inner-city residents in Detroit about different kinds of natural areas. They used a photo sort, asking respondents to rate 26 photos and then to describe the elements that led them to like or dislike a particular photo. Most said that they found outdoor environments relaxing and enjoyable; a substantial number said that being outdoors helped them escape worries and have some time to think. Most respondents expressed a preference for more neatly manicured areas than for areas with dense and "disorderly" vegetation. The study didn't reveal any significant differences based on demographic variables such as age or gender. The authors noted that this study demonstrates that inner-city Black residents value nature, but that the kinds of nature most preferred were landscapes that were well-manicured, open, with little underbrush, and with built facilities such as benches and paths. However, respondents who had previously lived outside the city were less likely to dislike the photos of landscapes with overgrown or disorderly vegetation. The authors suggested that urban planners should take these concerns into account when designing public parks.

Keywords: Environmental psychology, parks, urban planning, vegetation preferences.

98. Ulrich, R. 1984. View through a window may influence recovery from surgery. Science. 224: 420–421.

Ulrich's study measuring how vegetation affects patient recovery in hospital settings was a seminal article for environmental psychology research about human-nature interactions. He used a retrospective longitudinal experimental design by using data from a Pennsylvania hospital's records for the period 1972 to 1981 to compare recovery data for 46 cholecystectomy patients, 23 of whom had wall views and 23 of whom had views of trees from their windows. Patients with tree views had shorter hospital stays after surgery, required less pain medication, and had fewer postsurgery complications. Ulrich concluded that having a view of trees had a measurable restorative effect on these patients, but he cautioned that comparisons with a built environment more interesting than a blank wall are needed to sift out whether complexity or naturalness are the more important factors.

Keywords: Environmental psychology, human health, well-being.

99. Wells, N.M. 2000. At home with nature: effects of greenness on children's cognitive functioning. Environment and Behavior. 32(6): 775–795.

Wells examined the effect of greater exposure to vegetation on the cognitive functioning of low-income children in public housing environments. The study compared parents' assessment of their children's cognitive function and attention-focusing ability while living in substandard housing and then a year later after having moved into new single family dwellings. Data were obtained from parents of 17 children. The location of the study is not specified. Wells developed a naturalness scale based on the amount of vegetation visible from windows and present in the yard to compare the greenness of the pre- and post-move housing environments. A hierarchical regression analysis was performed to measure the relationship between naturalness of the environment and the children's directed attention capacity scores, with change in housing quality being taken into account. The greatest increase in directed attention capacity scores occurred in children who experienced the greatest increase in their home environment's naturalness scores, lending support to the hypothesis that natural settings have a positive influence on children's ability to focus their attention. However, additional research is needed to determine how much of the increase in naturalness scores was attributable to the children having "greener" views and how much was due to the children having the opportunity to play in more heavily vegetated surroundings. The research highlights the health benefits associated with trees and other vegetation in urban areas, and points to the importance of policies that encourage the preservation of existing trees, the planting of new trees, and the expansion of ground-level vegetation in and around public housing complexes.

Keywords: Environmental psychology, human health.

Environmental Health

The environmental health literature highlights the need for urban gathering studies to take into account the biochemical characteristics of existing and potential gathering sites. This vast literature documents the presence of toxins in urban soils and water bodies and varying levels of air pollution in many cities (Carvalho et al. 2005, Clark et al. 2006, Griffith et al. 2009). Soil contaminants are of particular concern as many nontimber forest products are used for foods or medicine and field guides indicate gathering may take place near diverse types of hardscape infrastructure (e.g., roads, railroads). The environmental health literature discusses the risks various soil contaminants pose to human health (Finster et al. 2003, Intawongse and Dean 2006). However, it also indicates the extent to which adsorption of toxins differs greatly by plant or fungal species (Finster et al. 2003, Intawongse and Dean 2006). Plants also differ in where they store chemicals that are toxic to humans (Finster et al. 2003). Most of this research focuses on common garden vegetables and fruits. However, Carvalho et al. (2005) looked at differences in heavy metal uptake in wild mushrooms, and Itoh et al. (2007) compared the elemental composition of wild and domestic plants.

Environmental health studies emphasize that levels of soil toxicity and air pollution are unevenly distributed and are influenced by both historical and current land and water uses (Carvalho et al. 2005, Clark et al. 2006, Finster et al. 2003). This literature points to the importance of incorporating geographic information system-based analyses of the distribution of toxics and pollutants into urban gathering research; the need for understanding which plants and plant parts people gather are likely to have environmental toxins in concentrations that pose risks to human health; and the rules (informal and formal) and types of local ecological knowledge that govern gathering practices relative to these geographies.

100. Carvalho, M.L.; Pimentel, A.C.; Fernandes, B. 2005. Study of heavy metals in wild edible mushrooms under different pollution conditions by x-ray fluorescence spectrometry. Analytical Sciences. 21: 747–750.

Compares the metal uptake in seven edible mushrooms relative to pollution conditions. The three pollution conditions examined included heavy automobile traffic, soil pollution linked to the use of pesticides and fertilizers in former vineyards, and incineration of hospital wastes. The sampling sites were in the Douro Valley in Portugal. At some sites, soil was collected in addition to mushrooms. Samples were analyzed by using x-ray fluorescence. High levels of copper and iron were found in some species in former vineyards. These findings are likely attributable to the persistence of residues of sulfate applied to control pests in previous decades. In areas near highways, lead contamination was 10 times higher than in other areas. Mushrooms collected at sites where hospital wastes had been incinerated were not contaminated with heavy metals.

Keywords: Environmental health, heavy metals, soil toxicity.

101. Clark, H.; Brabander, D.J.; Erdil, R.M. 2006. Sources, sinks, and exposure pathways of lead in urban garden soil. Journal of Environmental Quality. 35: 2066–2074.

This article found increased levels of lead in backyard gardens of members of The Food Project, a garden project in Roxbury and Dorchester, Massachusetts. The lead came from sources such as wind-blown lead particulates from leaded gasoline and from lead paint. The authors concluded, however, that gardeners risk greater exposure to lead through their drinking water than through their produce. They noted that the rapid screening procedures used to assess lead levels in their study make it feasible to conduct similar studies across large-scale areas.

Keywords: Environmental health, soil toxicity, toxics.

102. Finster, M.E.; Gray, K.A.; Binns, H.J. 2003. Lead levels of edibles grown in contaminated residential soils: a field survey. The Science of the Total Environment. 20: 1–13.

Examines levels of lead concentrations in urban garden soils and crops. It focuses especially on measuring contaminants in the edible portion of plants produced from two study sites in Chicago. Plants tested in the study included fruits, fruiting vegetables, leafy vegetables and herbs, and root vegetables. Both roots and shoots were tested for all plants. A total of 87 produce samples were obtained from 17 different properties distributed across the two study sites. Soil lead concentrations varied from 27 to 4,580 parts per million (ppm), with a median concentration of 800 ppm. The Environmental Protection Agency soil lead hazard cut-off values for soils in yards are 400 ppm for play areas and 1,200 ppm for nonplay areas. The authors found that all of the plants sampled accumulated lead to some extent but that concentrations of lead were much less detectable in fruiting parts of the plants and highest in the leaves. They concluded that eating plants from contaminated soils poses a potential hazard, depending on the type of plant and the part of the plant consumed. They recommended that urban gardeners have soils in prospective garden areas tested for lead, locate gardens away from buildings (which might have peeling paint), and avoid planting root or leafy vegetables in contaminated soils.

Keywords: Environmental health, soil toxicity, toxics.

103. Griffith, D.A.; Johnson, D.L.; Hunt, A. 2009. The geographic distribution of metals in urban soils: the case of Syracuse, NY. GeoJournal. 74: 275–291.

The objective of this research was to better understand the geographic distribution of metal contaminants across urban areas. Most previous research has focused on superfund sites. This study focuses on Syracuse, New York. Using 3,627 soil samples, the researchers used x-ray fluorescence to measure levels of 15 metals by using inductively coupled plasma spectroscopy. The distribution of the metal contaminants was compared to a nonurban landscape (a nearby river flood plain). The distribution of the metal contaminants was also aggregated by census block group and census tract. Lead levels were found to be both higher and more variable in Syracuse compared with the flood plain. Zinc levels were higher in the flood plain, but the variability in both landscapes was similar. Older housing and perhaps the presence of adolescents seem to be covariant with lead and zinc contamination. Newer, owner-occupied homes seem to be covariant with rubidium and zirconium contamination. This research recognizes a gap in the literature in understanding urban metal contamination, a topic highly relevant to urban foraging.

Keywords: Environmental health, heavy metals, soil toxicity, toxics.

104. Intawongse, M.; Dean, J.R. 2006. Uptake of heavy metals by vegetable plants grown on contaminated soil and their bioavailability in the human gastrointestinal tract. Food Additives and Contaminants. 23(1): 36–48.

This research sought to understand the effects of contaminated soils on vegetable crops by measuring heavy metal concentrations of lettuce, spinach, radishes, and carrots grown in compost containing cadmium, copper, manganese, lead, and zinc. Total metal concentrations in the plants were determined from their roots and leaves by using various spectroscopy techniques. The results showed that the uptake of cadmium, copper, manganese, and zinc corresponded to increasing soil concentration, whereas uptake of lead was low. Individual plant types differed in their metal uptake. There was no significant correlation between concentration and root versus leaf matter.

Keywords: Environmental health, heavy metals, soil toxicity, toxics.

105. Itoh, J.; Saitoh, Y.; Futatsugawa, S.; Ishii, K.; Sera, K. 2007. Elemental analysis of edible plants in natural environment: trace elements in wild plants. International Journal of Particle-Induced X-Ray Emission (PIXE). 17(3/4): 119–127.

Examines the concentration of various harmful and beneficial elements in wild plants. These plants were collected in Iwate prefecture in Japan. Levels of iron, copper, and zinc were found to be similar for wild plants and market vegetables. Wild plants had the same or lower levels of toxic elements such as chromium and lead as vegetables in the market. Additionally Itoh et al. found that the concentration of heavy metals in wild plants did not directly reflect the heavy metal concentrations of the soils in which they grew.

Keywords: Environmental health, heavy metals, nutrition, soil toxicity, toxics.

Urban Ecology

Urban ecologists examine the socioecological structures and functions of urban and urbanizing ecosystems. In the past decade, urban ecologists have focused their attention on developing conceptual models and research methods appropriate for gathering data about and analyzing coupled human-natural systems (Alberti et al. 2003, Grove and Burch 1997, Pickett et al. 1997). Much urban ecology research takes ecological concepts developed through the study of ecosystems with (assumed) limited human impact and applies them to urban ecosystems. For example, many urban ecologists specifically use the concepts of patch dynamics and gradients in their work to capture spatial patterns associated with, and degrees of, human alteration (e.g., Pickett et al. 1997). This transfer of concepts raises some process questions, such as, "What is the best way to add humans to ecological concepts that often intentionally did not include humans when they were originally developed?" To the extent that these models adequately address human practices and institutions, they can provide an effective framework for research on urban nontimber forest products. The social ecology approach put forth by Grove and Burch (1997), which pays particular attention to how ecological benefits and costs are both socially and spatially distributed, is particularly promising as an approach for research on urban gatherers.

Urban ecology studies that look at questions of distribution and access to green space, biological diversity, and tree types are of particular relevance to urban gathering research (Barbosa et al. 2007, Hope et al. 2006, Turner et al. 2004, Whitney and Adams 1980). Access to vegetation is a key concern for gatherers, and the composition, structure, and distribution of vegetation all shape whether and where desired species and products will be available in sufficient quantities for gathering. Also of interest to urban gathering research are the techniques urban ecologists have developed for analyzing species composition and vegetation structures by using hyperspectral satellite and LIDAR imagery analysis. As these techniques are refined, it will become possible to develop land use categorizations at the very fine scale required for mapping the interstitial spaces that appear to be important sources of products for urban gatherers (see Gabriel 2006, Hurley et al. 2008, and Jahnige 2002 in the urban gathering section).

Much urban ecology research discusses the (often negative) environmental impacts caused by humans; it rarely discusses humans as consumers of urban forest products. Kobori and Primack's (2003) account of the use of gathering as a strategy for restoring Tokyo's endangered anthropogenic satoyama forest habitat is a rare exception to urban ecologists' silence on gathering. Their work suggested that under some circumstances, managers might find that they can accomplish ecological goals through the strategic encouragement of certain types of gathering (see also Terada et al. 2010 under the urban forestry section). Finally, McDaniel and Alley's (2005) study, which found a correlation between participation in interactive outdoor activities and high local ecological knowledge scores, highlighted the need for similar studies comparing local ecological knowledge scores of gatherers and nongatherers.

106. Alberti, M.; Marzluff, J.M.; Shulenberger, E.; Bradley, G.; Ryan, C.; Zumbrunnen, C. 2003. Integrating humans into ecology: opportunities and challenges for studying urban ecosystems. BioScience. 53(12): 1169–1179.

Describes the properties of urban ecosystems and argues that humans need to be included as components of ecological analyses as they add selection pressures at all spatial and many temporal scales. Urban ecologists now think of cities as emergent, complex ecological entities and change in these systems is influenced by global as well as local drivers. The authors stressed the need to see human and ecological patterns as products of socioeconomic processes interacting with biophysical processes. Additionally, urbanization is multidimensional and variable over time and space. The authors proposed a model for urban ecology research that calls for looking at four elements: (1) the forces that drive urbanization, (2) the patterns that emerge on the land from the interaction of these forces, (3) how these patterns affect ecosystem function and human behavior, and (4) how ecosystem and human processes operate as feedback mechanisms. By using this model, researchers can identify the forces that drive urbanization, the patterns that emerge on the land, how these patterns affect ecosystem function and human behavior, and how ecosystem and human processes operate as feedback mechanisms. The authors recommended using complex adaptive systems theory for analyzing how urban structures and processes evolve over time through many local interactions at small scales among many agents. They concluded that urban ecosystem management requires interdisciplinarity and two-way communication between policy and science.

Keywords: Research framework, urban ecology.

107. Barbosa, O.; Tratalos, J.A.; Armsworth, P.R.; Davies, R.G.; Fuller, R.A.; Johnson, P.; Gaston, K.J. 2007. Who benefits from access to green space? A case study from Sheffield, U.K. Landscape and Urban Planning. 83: 187–195.

Looks at green spaces within cities, focusing on the distribution and access to green spaces within the city of Sheffield, United Kingdom. The authors measured the distance and access to both public and private green spaces for Sheffield residents, and how access varies among different socioeconomic and demographic sectors. The authors mapped all green spaces by using aerial photographs and survey maps, and calculated the distance to the nearest green space by using road network data. Ten socioeconomic and demographic groups were analyzed by using Experian's Mosaic United Kingdom demographic database. These groups were ranked based on deprivation, wealth, and age. Results showed that wealthier households had to travel longer distances to public green spaces, but had more access to private green spaces. Although wealthier households tended to have greater access to private green spaces (i.e., backyards), these spaces do not provide the same opportunities for social interaction and integration as public spaces. They are also more vulnerable to conversion into developed lots, and thus may be less persistent over the long term. The authors recommended that future research look more closely at how green spaces are actually used by residents, as this may not be purely based on distance, but could also be due to other factors such as the quality of green spaces.

Keywords: Environmental justice, green space, parks, urban ecology, urban planning.

108. Grove, J.M.; Burch, W.R., Jr. 1997. A social ecology approach and applications of urban ecosystem and landscape analyses: a case study of Baltimore, Maryland. Urban Ecosystems. 1: 259–275.

Articulates a model for integrating social components into urban ecosystem studies. The authors situated the study of urban ecology within the social sciences into historical perspective, tracing its origins to work by human ecology scholars (known as the Chicago School) carried out in the early 20th century. However, these human ecology scholars used ecology as a metaphor and did not actually look at how humans, plants, and animals integrated with each other. The late 1990s saw a new interest in looking at the flows and cycles of resources, social as well as biological, as well as at the biological and social mechanisms for allocating those resources within ecosystems that include humans. This analytical framework, which provides the framework for research in the Baltimore Long Term Ecological Research program, allows one to look at interactions at multiple scales, and to understand patterns of variability, resilience, and persistence. By using spatial analysis of land cover types and sociodemographics, they found that communities with higher income levels are more likely to have trees and grass. They attributed this to inequities in "green" investment by both the private market and the government. They concluded that the kinds of measures ecologists use for measuring other communities (population characteristics, patterns and processes, diets, time budgets, health, and actuarial dynamics) can also be used to measure human communities.

Keywords: Research framework, social ecology, urban ecology.

109. Hope, D.; Gries, C.; Casagrande, D.; Redman, C.L.; Grimm, N.B.; Martin, C. 2006. Drivers of spatial variation in plant diversity across the Central Arizona-Phoenix ecosystem. Society and Natural Resources. 19: 101–116.

Compares plant species diversity and composition in the Phoenix metropolitan area to the surrounding desert, looking at the relative importance of socioeconomic variables (such as land use history; social, economic, cultural, and technological factors) in determining spatial variability of the vegetation. They used a probability-based sampling approach to distinguish the social and biophysical variables that influence vegetation diversity. The biophysical variables used in this study include elevation, latitude, longitude, distance from urban center, population density, distance to the nearest freeway, soil nitrate levels, land use cover, percentage of impervious surface, and history of agricultural use. Socioeconomic variables used were median household income, past and current land use, and median housing age. Results showed that urban plots had higher levels of diversity and about twice as many exotic species as desert sites. Diversity at urban sites was explained best by land use, family income (increased diversity with increased household income up to $50,750), and past agricultural use (lower diversity where past agricultural use removed native vegetation). The authors point out that as wealth increases, residents inhabit landscapes with higher plant diversity, either through preference or planting. The authors recommended that future research further explore the wealth-diversity relationships, such as factors that influence individual decisionmaking around plant diversity.

Keywords: Biodiversity, social ecology, urban ecology.

110. Kobori, H.; Primack, R.B. 2003. Participatory conservation approaches for satoyama, the traditional forest and agricultural landscape of Japan. Ambio. 32(4): 307–311.

Kobori and Primack described efforts to restore Japan's satoyama forests, an anthropogenic landscape mosaic composed of forests, rice paddies, dry rice fields, grasslands, and water courses. This mixed landscape provides a variety of habitats for wildlife and plants and is critical habitat for a number of rare and endangered insect and floral species. Human activities, such as harvesting fallen leaves for fertilizer, cutting grass, and harvesting wood, are essential for maintaining several species of threatened wildflowers as well as these and other flowers on which the rare and endangered insect species depend. Over the past half-century, the transition out of farming and a shift from wood to coal and oil as the main heat source for homes has led to the deterioration of the satoyama woodlands. An effort to restore the woodlands in the Sayama Hills on Tokyo's periphery began in the early 1990s and involves planting seedlings, mowing grass, and harvesting trees. Another conservation effort in the city of Yokohama is being carried out as a partnership between the local university and citizen volunteers. Among other activities, the harvesting of bamboo and bamboo shoots is an important aspect of this effort to restore the satoyama landscape. The Sayama Hills and Yokohama conservation efforts indicate that the harvest of urban nontimber forest products and biodiversity conservation can be mutually compatible.

Keywords: Biodiversity, conservation, ecological restoration, sustainability, urban ecology, urban gathering, volunteers.

111. McDaniel, J.; Alley, K.D. 2005. Connecting local environmental knowledge and land use practices: a human ecosystem approach to urbanization in West Georgia. Urban Ecosystems. 8: 23–38.

Examines the loss of local environmental knowledge (LEK) associated with urbanization. The researchers compared LEK along a variety of social dimensions (gender, income, education, and participation in various outdoor activities) in three places (rural, urban, and developing areas) in west Georgia through a close-ended survey of 447 residents in two counties. The researchers looked at how these data correlated with land use practices. People living in managed pine watersheds had the highest average LEK scores, whereas those living in urban areas had the lowest. Active participants in outdoor recreation (especially bird watching) had the highest LEKs. Timber owners and landowners who participated in streamside management activities had higher LEK scores than other survey participants. The study suggests that proximity to natural environments and more interactive types of engagement with natural environments are associated with greater levels of LEK.

Keywords: Ecological knowledge, urban ecology.

112. Pickett, S.T.A.; Burch, W.R.J.; Dalton, S.E.; Forsman, T.W.; Grove, J.M.; Rowntree, R. 1997. A conceptual framework for the study of human ecosystems in urban areas. Urban Ecosystems. 1: 185–199.

Describes a framework for studying urban ecosystems that seeks to satisfy both natural and social scientists. This framework is based on an expansive definition of urban that includes cities, suburbs, exurbs, and rural hinterlands of cities. The authors proposed a dynamic model capable of including many social components and that can account for hierarchies of wealth, education, and power at different spatial scales. Their model acknowledges the existence of social and spatial heterogeneity in the distribution of wealth, knowledge, status, territory, and power. Patch dynamics can be used to describe human ecological systems and how they change over time as different social groups occupy particular spaces. The authors noted that the classical ecosystem approach is to look at fluxes in matter and energy, focusing attention on flows of nutrients, toxins, wastes, and energy. In contrast, the patch-dynamics approach focuses attention on the "cause, structure, and change of spatial patterns and the processes that are affected by the spatial dynamics (Pickett et al. 1997: 192). Combining these two approaches (flows and patch dynamics) allows for much more powerful studies of ecosystem change.

Keywords: Research framework, social ecology, urban ecology.

113. Shandas, V. 2007. An empirical study of streamside landowners' interest in riparian conservation. Journal of the American Planning Association. 73(2): 173–184.

Shandas conducted a survey of households in the Seattle area with land adjacent to riparian areas to determine their vegetation preferences and vegetation management behavior on those parcels. Surveys were mailed to all 667 households in the area with homes along streams; however, only 272 responded. Only those who owned their homes were included in the analysis. The survey included photographs of different types of riparian vegetation, which respondents were asked to rank in order of preference. Shandas used geographic information system software to calculate the total area in vegetation for each parcel so that he could compare the landowner's stated preferences with the actual vegetation on the parcel. Among the respondents, photos with more vegetation received higher ratings than those with moderate or no vegetation. However, the actual amount of vegetation on their parcels tended to be much lower than on the photos that received higher rankings. Answers to open-ended questions on the survey indicated that the disconnect between stated preferences for and actual amounts of vegetation on properties could be linked to three factors. These included lack of clarity about what actions were permitted along the streams, fears about negative impacts of making changes to their parcels, and the cost and time it would take to make changes. Additionally, landowners expressed a high level of distrust about information from government agencies. Shandas suggested that planners clarify land use ordinances to make them more understandable to property owners. He also suggested that when making land use policies and decisions, that planning agencies take into account landowners' ecological knowledge.

Keywords: Conservation, stewardship, urban planning, vegetation preferences, yards.

114. Turner, W.R.; Nakamura, T.; Dinetti, M. 2004. Global urbanization and the separation of humans from nature. BioScience. 54(6): 585–590.

Measured biodiversity in urban areas as a proxy indicator of how much contact humans have with nature. The researchers used human census data and data on birds and ferns from five cities (Tucson, Arizona; Berlin, Germany; Washington, D.C.; Florence, Italy; Chiba City, Japan) to see whether and how biodiversity levels differed with population density. The study showed that most people in all of the cities except Chiba City lived in areas with lower than average biodiversity. The study's overall conclusion is that most of the world's urban population lives in biological poverty. This means that most people are experiencing poor ecological conditions and that over time, those conditions will become normalized. Additionally, because studies show that human health is linked to presence of vegetation, the lack of biodiversity affects human health negatively. The authors noted that city structure as well as population density affects the extent to which humans are exposed to biodiversity. For example, residents in the much more densely populated city of Berlin have access to greater biodiversity than residents of the less densely populated Tucson. The authors concluded that because it is unlikely that dispersing people away from urban areas will be beneficial for the environment, it would be better for policies to focus on increasing biodiversity within urban areas.

Keywords: Biodiversity, human health, sustainability, urban ecology.

115. Whitney, G.G.; Adams, S.D. 1980. Man as maker of new plant communities. Journal of Applied Ecology. 17: 431–448.

Whitney and Adams used ordination techniques coupled with correlation analysis and an overlay of socioeconomic variables to identify the major factors contributing to the observed distribution of vegetative complexes in Akron, Ohio. They used 1970 Census data for income, education, and age of the development, with analysis taking place at the census tract and block levels. They used a purposive sampling strategy structured to capture the likely range of variation across the city. Data were gathered on species and size of ornamental and shade trees in front lawns. Ordination along with reciprocal averaging was used to categorize sites according to size and species. Five major complexes emerged from this analysis: old oak, mixed suburban, conifer, maple, and inner city. The old oak and mixed suburban complexes tended to occur in more recently developed sites and where residents had higher incomes, higher house values, and more education. The conifer complex was associated with blue collar residential areas, and the inner city complex tended to occur in older areas of the city and where income and educational levels were lower on average. Fruit trees were an important component of the inner city complex, but much less common in the other complexes. Whitney and Adams speculated that the high percentage of fruit trees in the inner city may be linked to the influx of African Americans from the rural south during and after World War Two. They concluded that urban vegetation patterns needed to be viewed as products of both cultural and biophysical processes.

Keywords: Cultural practices, urban ecology, yards.

Urban Forestry

Within the vast literature on urban forestry, research on urban forest assessments, tree preference studies, and community forestry have particular relevance for gathering-related research and policy. Urban forest assessments describe the current status of the urban forest including species composition, spatial distribution, and health (McPherson et al. 2008); others also assign monetary values to the different services urban forests provide (Donovan and Butry 2010, Nowack et al. 2006). Such assessments play an important role in garnering support and funding for tree-planting campaigns, open-space reserves, and basic maintenance of "green infrastructure" in urban areas. However, we located no assessments that included economic or cultural values of harvested products such as fruits, nuts, wood, or leaves. By excluding nontimber forest products (NTFPs) from consideration, the assessments omit a significant value of urban forests. Their exclusion means that policymakers and planners are unlikely to take NTFPs or the concerns of the people who gather them into account when developing or revising policies and management plans. Urban gathering research structured in ways that produced data that could be integrated into urban forest valuation models would not only help inform urban NTFP policymaking but would also improve the accuracy and relevance of these assessments.

Tree preference studies, which often apply methods and theoretical frameworks from environmental psychology, seek to understand the types, forms, and placement of trees humans prefer, as well as how preferences differ along racial, gender, age, land tenure, and other socioeconomic dimensions (Elmendorf et al. 2005, Fraser and Kennedy 2000, Lohr et al. 2004, Schroeder et al. 2006). Where urban forest assessments seek to measure the value of urban forests to communities as a whole, tree preference studies typically are structured to measure the value of urban trees to individuals. Additionally, Wolf's (2003) research suggested that streetscape vegetation influences consumer purchasing patterns and perceptions about businesses. Data from such studies often guide urban forest planning and extension programming. Among the articles we reviewed, availability of NTFPs does not figure prominently among the reasons why householders prefer or dislike particular tree species. However, the lack of mention of NTFPs may be due to use of close-ended questionnaires in which NTFPs are not included among the options. One NTFP that does show up in some studies is fruit. Householder views on fruit, however, are ambivalent. Barker (1986) stated that many householders see fruit as potential "litter" and consider fruit trees as problems. Fraser and Kenney (2000) found that householders in Italian and Portuguese neighborhoods in Toronto greatly preferred fruit trees over shade trees. By contrast, householders of British descent preferred shade trees over fruit trees.

Urban community forestry research points to the social benefits of vegetation (Kuo 2003) as well as to the individual and social benefits associated with active involvement in tree-planting, restoration, and other urban forestry activities (Westphal 2003). Like tree preference studies, much of this work draws on theories and methods of environmental psychology. The recent resurgence in urban agriculture also has brought community gardens within the purview of urban community forestry (see Svendsen 2009 in the urban planning section). Efforts to restore Tokyo's satoyama forest rely heavily on community input, and Terada et al. (2010) found that reintroducing traditional coppicing practices along with the use of thinned wood for fuel has the potential to reconnect humans with nature while reducing carbon emissions.

Although the urban forestry literature is virtually silent on gathering and the sociocultural values of urban forest products, it nonetheless provides concepts and research methods that can inform urban gathering studies. Westphal's (2003) social benefits framework, for example, can be used to evaluate urban gathering policies. For example, a question that one might ask is "What benefits accrue to individuals, organizations, and neighborhoods when gathering of fruits and nuts is permitted in city parks?" Kuo (2003) found that greenery around public housing attracted a more diverse set of people outdoors, creating an informal surveillance network that reduced crime. As mentioned earlier, this finding raises the question of whether the presence of gatherers in parks might also function as an informal surveillance network that enhances public safety in city parks.

Tree preference studies also have some important lessons for urban gathering research and policy. For example, given that cultural background appears to affect tree preferences (Fraser and Kenney 2000, Schroeder et al. 2006), it is likely that cultural background also shapes which products (and tree species) are preferred. Such preferences may also differ along other socioeconomic dimensions such as race, age, gender, and educational level. Urban gathering research thus needs to be designed in ways that can determine whether such differences exist. In addition, urban forest policies should be developed through processes in which an appropriately diverse set of gatherers participate as stakeholders.

116. Barker, P.A. 1986. Fruit litter from urban trees. Journal of Arboriculture. 12(12): 293–298.

Barker had a negative view of fruit trees, noting that their litter is a major problem for householders in urban areas, who are typically responsible for maintaining sidewalk and street easements. He discussed examples of two common "problem" fruit trees, American sweetgum (*Liquidambar styraciflua*) and Lavelle hawthorn (*Crataegus x. lavallei*), two species commonly found in urban areas. Sweetgums are frequently planted in yards, but their fruits are tough and get caught up in mowers. Hawthorns are often planted adjacent to streets, and their soft, red-orange fruits fall onto sidewalks, creating a safety hazard (slipping) as well as staining carpets. He argued that the remedies for fruit litter are unsatisfactory, and therefore householders are ambivalent about the planting and presence of fruit trees even though they appreciate the shade these trees provide. He recommended that urban foresters select nonfruiting tree varieties for street tree plantings.

Keywords: Street trees, urban forestry.

117. Donovan, G.H.; Butry, D.T. 2010. Trees in the city: valuing street trees in Portland, Oregon. Landscape and Urban Planning. 94(2):77–83.

This research sought to determine the effect of street trees on sales prices and time on market of houses in Portland, Oregon. Researchers collected onsite and remote data about each of the 3,479 house sales on the east side of Portland between July 2006 and April 2007. By using the hedonistic price method, the researchers found that the presence of street trees added $8,870 to the sales price and reduced time on the market by 1.7 days. Benefits also spill over to neighboring houses. The article discusses the distribution of responsibilities for tree upkeep, which in Portland is largely the responsibility of the landowner adjacent to the street strip. Although the paper discusses shading and other benefits of the urban forest, nontimber forest products, urban foraging, and fruit use are not discussed.

Keywords: Street trees, urban forestry, valuation.

118. Elmendorf, W.F.; Willits, F.K.; Sasidharan, V.; Godbey, G. 2005. Urban park and forest participation and landscape preference: a comparison between blacks and whites in Philadelphia and Atlanta. U.S. Journal of Arboriculture. 31(6): 318–326.

Reports the findings of a comparative study of the use and preferences of Black and White users of public urban open spaces in Philadelphia, Pennsylvania, and Atlanta, Georgia. Data were gathered through surveys in Philadelphia (300 respondents) and Atlanta (359 respondents). The researchers measured frequency of park visitation, whether respondents thought urban open spaces were beneficial, and the types of activities respondents participated in while in the park. Landscape preferences and willingness to volunteer also were measured. They found that Blacks were less likely to agree that "nature" amenities were important, but more Blacks than Whites thought that "traditional park" landscapes and recreational facilities were important. The authors concluded that differences exist between Blacks and Whites regarding their participation, preferences, and perceptions of urban open spaces, a finding that is consistent with other studies. They emphasized that the differences observed in the study argue for park managers to pay attention to ensuring there is not discrimination in terms of making decisions about what park landscapes will look like.

Keywords: Parks, urban forestry, vegetation preferences.

119. Fraser, E.D.G.; Kenney, W.A. 2000. Cultural background and landscape history as factors affecting perceptions of the urban forest. Journal of Arboriculture. 26(2): 106–113.

Compares attitudes toward trees among four ethnic communities in the city of Toronto, Canada. By using a list of names for household heads interviewed in the 1991 Canadian census, Fraser and Kenney selected prospective respondents whose last names indicated a strong likelihood that they were of British, Chinese, Italian, or Portuguese descent. Potential interviewees were randomly selected from each of the ethnic groups. A total of 210 residents participated in the survey. In addition to face-to-face interviews, the research team inventoried the vegetation on the respondent's property. The authors found that householders of British origin were most likely to have and appreciate shade trees; householders of Chinese origin were least likely to have and appreciate either fruit or shade trees. Yard owners of Italian and Portuguese origin were most likely to have or appreciate fruit trees and vegetable gardens and were uninterested in having shade trees when they conflicted with their gardens.

Keywords: Cultural practices, immigrants, urban forestry, vegetation preferences, yards.

120. Konijnendijk, C. 2008. The forest and the city: the cultural landscape of urban woodland. New York: Springer. 245 p.

Konijnendijk examines urban forests as cultural landscapes drawing extensively on examples from northern Europe but also including illustrative examples from cities around the globe. He noted that cities and forests have long been linked, often in mutually beneficial relationships. He provided examples of the multiple and frequently overlapping roles of urban forests in human lives, such as improving human emotional and spiritual well-being, providing opportunities for recreation and physical exercise, and improving the aesthetic qualities of urban environments. Konijkendijk calls attention to the importance of urban forests as sources of products, devoting an entire chapter to examples of the variety of products, such as wood, berries, and mushrooms humans derive from woodlands in and around cities.

Keywords: Gathering, human health, policy, urban forestry, well-being.

121. Kuo, F. 2003. The role of arboriculture in a healthy social ecology. Journal of Arboriculture. 29(3): 148–155.

Kuo draws on defensible space theory to examine the relationship between the presence of vegetation and social ecosystem health in inner city Chicago. Defensible space theory posits that physical features of neighborhoods affect community strength and crime rates by influencing informal contacts among people and increasing informal surveillance. Kuo argued that by extension, if the presence of trees and grass draws people to use spaces, then their presence should have a positive effect on public safety. She summarized findings from a series of large-scale studies conducted in Chicago to support her argument. These studies used a variety of methods including photo simulations and respondent reports of their behavior. She found that green cover was linked to greater and more positive social interactions in residential outdoor space. Kuo also found that residents who interacted more were more likely to share resources. She argued that by strengthening social ties among residents, the presence of trees contributed to the expansion of social networks. Kuo concluded that urban foresters need to integrate trees into residential areas if they wish to maximize the social benefits of trees.

Keywords: Crime, environmental psychology, human health, social benefits, urban forestry.

122. Lohr, V.I.; Pearson-Mims, C.H.; Tarnai, J.; Dilllman, D.A. 2004. How urban residents rate and rank the benefits and problems associated with trees in cities. Journal of Arboriculture. 30(1): 28–35.

Looks at how beliefs and attitudes about trees are related to the care, management, and protection of trees. Lohr et al. conducted a nationwide phone survey of about 2000 adults. They found that people gave the highest ratings to shading and cooling functions of trees. Other benefits that received high ratings included calming functions and air and noise pollution reduction. The study did not include gathering of products on the list of benefits. Annoyances related to trees that were rated the highest included allergy effects and the blocking of street and business signs. However, in general, respondents had difficulty ranking the annoyances of trees. More than 80 percent of the respondents stated that trees were important to their quality of life. Although there was some difference in responses by race, none were significant, and all categories felt trees contributed positively to their quality of life.

Keywords: Urban forestry, vegetation preferences.

123. McPherson, E.G.; Simpson, J.R.; Xiao, Q.; Wu, C. 2008. Los Angeles 1-million tree canopy cover assessment. Gen. Tech. Rep. PSW-GTR-207. Albany, CA: U.S. Department of Agriculture, Forest Service, Pacific Southwest Research Station. 52 p.

Measured Los Angeles' existing tree canopy cover to determine whether there is space for an additional 1 million trees, as proposed under the Million Trees Los Angeles' initiative. The research also estimated future benefits from the plantings. Remote sensing data, aerial photographs, geographic information systems, and image-processing software were used in this research. These techniques classified land cover types, measured total canopy cover, and identified potential tree planting sites. Benefits were estimated by using data from previous studies and were applied to tree planting sites in Los Angeles. The study found that Los Angeles has 10.8 million trees. McPherson et al. identified 2.5 million potential tree-planting sites; however, they concluded that only 1.3 million of those sites could realistically be planted. Their data suggested the average annual benefit per tree is between $38 and

$56. Most of these benefits were classified as aesthetic or other. Stormwater runoff reduction, energy savings, air quality improvement, and atmospheric carbon reduction were also noted as benefits. Products derived from trees were not mentioned (or measured) in this study.

Keywords: Economic benefits, urban forestry, valuation.

124. Nowack, D.J.; Hoehn, R.E.I.; Crane, D.E.; Stevens, J.C.; Walton, J.T. 2006. Assessing urban forest effects and values: Minneapolis' urban forest. Res. Bull. NE-166. Newtown Square, PA: U.S. Department of Agriculture, Forest Service, Northeastern Research Station. 20 p.

Examined what urban forests contribute to local and regional societies and economies. The Northeastern Research Station of the USDA Forest Service developed the Urban Forest Effects (UFORE) model to understand the forest resource; improve urban forest policies, planning, and management; provide data; and determine how trees affect and enhance the environment. This study focused on Minneapolis, Minnesota. It determined values of the forest structure, risk of insect pests and diseases, air pollution removal, carbon storage, annual carbon sequestration, and changes in building energy use. Minneapolis' 979,000 trees remove 384 tons of air pollution annually, providing a service valued at $1.9 million. The trees sequester 8,900 tons of carbon annually, a service valued at $164,000. Trees in Minneapolis reduce energy costs in residential buildings by $221,000 annually, and reduce carbon emissions in those buildings by 900 tons, thus creating an additional $15,900 value. The replacement value of Minneapolis' urban forest is $756 million. The UFORE model does not include sociocultural values derived from trees.

Keywords: Economic benefits, urban forestry, valuation.

125. Schroeder, H.; Flannigan, J.; Coles, R. 2006. Residents' attitudes toward street trees in the U.K. and U.S. communities. Arboriculture and Urban Forestry. 32(5): 236–246.

Compares data about tree preferences from surveys in two communities in England with results of an earlier survey conducted in the Midwestern United States. Researchers received 130 useable surveys. The results showed very similar results on the overall opinion of trees in front of homes—generally good to excellent—in both U.K. and U.S. communities. Dominant reasons for liking street trees included that they were pleasing to the eye, they enhance the look of the garden and home, and that they bring nature closer to people. In the United Kingdom, autumn color was also listed as important. More communities mentioned falling leaves, seeds, and sticks as an annoyance in the United Kingdom, but still this was only a minor annoyance. United Kingdom residents had definite preference for smaller trees than residents in the United States. Tree products were not mentioned as a benefit. The researchers concluded the differences observed between the United States and United Kingdom are likely related to climate differences and the size and layout of homes (i.e., United Kingdom residents prefer smaller trees, are less likely to list shade as a benefit, and less likely to see debris as an annoyance than U.S. residents). The authors noted that arborists need to take these conditions into account when selecting species and locations for tree plantings.

Keywords: Cultural practices, street trees, urban forestry, vegetation preferences.

126. Terada, T.; Yokohari, M.; Bolthouse, J.; Tanaka, N. 2010. "Refueling" satoyama woodland restoration in Japan: enhancing restoration practice and experiences through woodfuel utilization. Nature and Culture. 5(3): 251–276.

Argues that ecological restoration requires paying attention to sociocultural values and identifying instances where productive uses of urban forests has net ecological and social benefits. The authors argued that volunteers alone cannot accomplish the work needed to restore Tokyo's satoyama woodlands, which provide habitat for a number of rare or endangered species. These woodlands are anthropogenic in their origins, created through centuries of complex and intensive human use of the landscape. In particular, regular coppicing of the oaks that dominate the satoyama woodlands to produce poles for fuel wood was an important component of this socioecological system. Very light thinning is currently done by volunteers as a recreational activity. However, the authors found that recreational thinning is insufficient to maintain satoyama woodlands. They conducted four restoration scenarios and found that traditional coppicing, which involves removing a much larger amount of wood than is currently removed through recreational thinning, had greater potential than the other three scenarios examined (ground cover removal, light thinning, and intensive thinning) to reduce carbon emissions. They recommended that urban ecological restoration place "greater emphasis on restoring mutually beneficial connections between people and nature."

Keywords: Conservation, ecological restoration, stewardship, sustainability, urban forestry, volunteers.

127. Westphal, L.M. 2003. Urban greening and social benefits: a study of empowerment outcomes. Journal of Arboriculture. 29(3): 137–147.

Westphal outlined a social benefits framework that urban planners can use in crafting urban greening programs. Her framework asks planners to examine three aspects of urban greening programs: (1) Who gets the benefits of green space? (2) What benefits do passive experiences with green space provide? And (3) What benefits accrue from active involvement in urban greening activities? She emphasized the need for planners to understand whether benefits accrue at the individual, organizational, and community level. She focused on the concept of empowerment, which she argued is often incorrectly applied to community forestry projects. By using photoelicitation and semistructured interviews, she examined the empowerment outcomes of a greening program implemented in Chicago during 1995. Respondents on four different blocks were asked to take photos of things on their block that had improved or gotten worse since the greening program. Respondents were also asked to discuss why they chose those items to photograph and what their views of the greening project were. Drawing on empowerment theory, she then analyzed the data to identify indicators of empowerment including efficacy, mastery, control, proactive behavior, and sense of competence. She found that in two cases, individuals associated with the project felt empowered but that the communities in which they lived did not become empowered. By contrast, empowerment in another block occurred at both the individual and block level. Westphal concluded that social benefits are not inevitable outcomes of urban greening projects and that to structure empowering projects, planners need to understand the social milieu in which the project takes place.

Keywords: Research framework, social benefits, urban forestry.

128. Wolf, K.L. 2003. Public response to the urban forest in inner-city business districts. Journal of Arboriculture. 29(3): 117–126.

Wolf evaluated how the presence of trees affects retail businesses located in revitalization districts. Previous research indicated that business owners tended to see trees as nuisances if not outright detrimental to their business. This study explored how street vegetation affected consumer perceptions of businesses in the area, whether vegetation influenced shopping behavior, and whether perceptions and behaviors differed by demographic categories. In a mail survey, residents of business revitalization districts in seven U.S. cities were provided with different vegetation scenarios and asked to describe their perceptions of those streetscapes and their willingness to pay for a specified set of goods and services from businesses located in each of the streetscapes. Wolf found that respondents gave higher visual quality and comfort ratings to scenarios with more trees; they also indicated a willingness to travel farther to shop in retail areas with trees. The author concluded that programs for planting and maintaining treescapes in business districts have the potential to positively affect consumer experiences and business revenues.

Keywords: Economic benefits, urban forestry, vegetation preferences.

129. Zube, E.H.; Kennedy, C.B. 1990. Urban forests in the desert? Journal of Arboriculture. 16(4): 95–98.

The authors conducted a mail survey of 192 Tucson residents to assess their attitudes toward street trees and their views about the values of trees. Street trees received a high average ranking for contributing to better quality of life. About 80 percent of the respondents indicated that they viewed trees as important for shading yards, 60 percent felt they were important for making a pleasant street environment, and 52 percent stated that trees contributed positively to the quality of the city. Authors concluded that there was only moderate support for street trees, but very strong support for yard trees that provide shade.

Keywords: Social benefits, street trees, urban forestry, vegetation preferences.

Urban Planning

The urban planning literature is expansive, with emphasis historically placed on issues of urban renewal, transportation planning, and growth management. Within these arenas, concerns about food issues were largely confined to discussions about agricultural land conservation, whereas discussions about nature tended to be wrapped up with a broad focus on open space or parks provision. Yet, intentionally or not, the plans and policies of municipalities long have variously hindered or promoted urban food production and urban gathering (Falck 2002, Howe 2002, Moore 2006). At the same time, early literature in urban planning and design emphasized the importance of integrating dynamics of the countryside into urban places and discussions of what today would best be described as green infrastructure (greenfrastructure). In the past decade, however, the urban planning literature has witnessed a renewed interest in, among other things, biodiversity in the city and a blossoming of concerns for issues surrounding urban sustainability (Berke 2008). Urban planning scholarship has a renewed and sustained focus on the role of parks and open space in contributing to the provision of ecosystem services and better quality of life (Berke 2008), as well as crime reduction (Blomley 2004) and physical fitness (Floyd et al. 2008).

Recent discussions on the role of green space in urban ecosystems have paved the way for work that (re)considers the role of local food and gardening as part of creating and maintaining sustainable cities (Stuart 2005, Svendsen 2009, Van Hassell 2005). Reintegrating the gathering of edible nontimber forest products into urban ecosystems, however, potentially challenges prevailing conceptions of public and private property and successful reintegration is likely to require the development of new institutions for managing streetscapes and other quasipublic spaces planted with edible species (see Nordahl 2009 in the urban gathering section). Blomley's (2004) work on greenways in Vancouver, British Columbia, for example, provides an interesting example of how informal tenure systems regulating access to tree products can emerge on publicly held lands.

Urban planners and landscape architects have pointed out the need for rethinking the "nature-as-backdrop" mentality that drives much current green space management. For example, Gobster (2007) called for ecological restoration programs that involve rather than exclude the public from restored green spaces. Similarly, Thompson (2002) argued for the importance of green spaces where children and adults can interact tactilely with natural processes. She limited her examples to children's play. Van Hassell (2005), Stuart (2005), and Svendsen (2009) provided similar examples in the context of community gardening. However, it is a short step to extend their conclusion to tactile interactions with nature through gathering. Indeed, as described in the urban gathering section, recent ecological restoration programs in Japan are already taking advantage of the human propensity for gathering to accomplish restoration and environmental education goals simultaneously (see Kobori and Primack 2003 in the urban forestry section).

The emerging literature in urban planning that considers greenfrastructure and sustainability in tandem suggests potential areas for fruitful engagement with work on gathering. For example, the literature on sustainable planning emphasizes the need for more vegetation in cities. However, a question yet to be adequately addressed is how and by whom this vegetation will be managed. For centuries if not millennia, gathering has been a practice by which humans inadvertently and intentionally shaped vegetated sites, patches, landscapes, and regions. Studies of urban gathering have the potential to identify gathering practices that could be productively integrated into greenfrastructure management as well as those that are inappropriate in particular socioecological contexts.

130. Berke, P.R. 2008. The evolution of green community planning, scholarship, and practice. Journal of the American Planning Association. 74(4): 393–407.

Examines how visions of urban form have influenced green communities. It examines secondary sources to describe main themes in green communities: harmony with natural systems, human health, spiritual well-being and renewal, livable built environments, and fair-share communities. Berke concluded that bioregionalism and other environmental ideas of the early 20th century did not take hold in planning practice. Although there is a demand for green communities, efforts to integrate green communities into conventional planning have not been satisfactory.

Keywords: Sustainability, urban planning.

131. Blomley, N. 2004. Un-real estate: proprietary space and public gardening. Antipode. 36(4): 614–641.

Blomley critiqued an urban planning practice known as crime prevention through environmental design (CPTED). This practice is based on Newman's concept of defensible space. This theory assumes that people will care for things over which they exercise proprietary control, and thus urban designs that tacitly extend private space into public space will encourage "natural" surveillance and reduce crime. Blomley called this "un-real space" as it is extra-legal in the sense that people exercise private control over what is legally public property. Blomley examined the use of CPTED on the Atlantic Street Greenway in a low income area of Vancouver, British Columbia. Methods included indepth interviews with 42 respondents, as well as participant observation. The goal of the Greenway was to transform what had been a high-crime "wild" space into a low-crime domesticated space by requiring the community to maintain the greenway. Although many residents referred to the greenway as "our" space, even those who invested a lot of time into maintaining it did not talk about it as "my" space. Many residents planted trees, but while other residents considered those trees as property of the person who had planted them, the space itself was considered neighborhood space. Interestingly, however, the fruits from privately planted trees were felt to belong to the planter and not to the community as a whole. Blomley concluded that greenways are important as spaces where community and citizenship are produced and that it is important to make streets into places that encourage the intertwining of public and private space.

Keywords: Crime, property regimes, urban planning, vegetation preferences.

132. Falck, Z.J.S. 2002. Controlling the weed nuisance in turn-of-the-century American cities. Environmental History. 7(4): 611–631.

Falck examined the emergence of weed control laws in late 19th and early 20th century American cities. In the developing urban landscapes of that era, weeds were ubiquitous, cropping up in vacant lots, along streets, and in many yards. Urban elites equated weeds with filth and disease, and believed that property owners who failed to control weeds were morally suspect and civically irresponsible. By the late 19th century, many cities had weed ordinances aimed at ensuring that property owners eradicated or at least minimized the weeds growing in their yards. Falck described a court case brought by the city of St. Louis against a property owner who refused to eradicate the sunflowers growing in his yard. City officials considered sunflowers a public health risk because they blocked the sun from reaching the soil, an action which was thought to promote soil pathogens. The defendant argued—unsuccessfully—that sunflowers were beneficial to human well-being. Enforcing weed ordinances, however, proved very difficult and costly with enforcement being most likely to occur in elite residential areas. Falck noted that weed control laws essentially codified notions about which plants were appropriate in urban spaces and who would control them. He concluded that weed control efforts played an important role in demarcating boundaries between civilized nature and wild nature, rich and poor neighborhoods, and safe and dangerous places.

Keywords: Environmental history, policy, urban planning, vegetation preferences, yards.

133. Floyd, M.F.; Spengler, J.O.; Maddock, J.E.; Gobster, P.H.; Suau, L.J. 2008. Park-based physical activity in diverse communities of two U.S. cities. American Journal of Preventative Medicine. 34(4): 299–305.

Considers how the design of public parks affects physical activity. It uses the ecologic model of health behavior to assess how changing built environments affects behavior. It assesses levels of physical activity in selected neighborhood parks in Chicago, Illinois and Tampa, Florida. The researchers compared physical activity levels of park users with different ethnic/racial and income compositions, and examined whether level of activity is associated with race/ethnicity or income. Methods include use of census block group data and geographic information systems to identify sample parks, and direct observation. Physical activity was measured by modifying the System for Observing Play and Leisure in Youth approach, categorizing observed individuals by age group, gender, park activity zone, and neighborhood racial/ethnic and income composition. Results showed that activity level for more than half of park users is sedentary, and suggests that the design of activity areas in parks can enhance physical activity.

Keywords: Environmental psychology, human health, parks, urban planning.

134. Gobster, P. 2007. Urban park restoration and the "museumification" of nature. Nature and Culture. 2(2): 96–114.

Gobster examined urban ecological restoration of city parks, drawing on his experiences in Chicago and San Francisco. He reviewed the evolution of natural experiences in urban parks, starting in the 18th century. He concluded that urban ecological restoration often results in a "museumification" that restricts interactions between people and nature to certain activities and experiences. The researcher argues that other types of management in urban green spaces may create better experiences for users while still encouraging ecological restoration. These include involving the public in the process of restoration, blurring the line between visitors and managers, and more generally increasing interaction with the environment.

Keywords: Green space, parks, urban planning.

135. Howe, J. 2002. Planning for urban food: the experience of two UK cities. Planning Practice and Research. 17(2): 125–144.

This comparative study of urban agriculture and green space policies for the cities of Leeds and Bradford explains the implications of urban agriculture for the planning system in the United Kingdom. Bradford has made efforts to develop policies related to urban food, whereas Leeds has made fewer efforts in these areas. Howe stated that there are barriers to how effective planning can be in promoting or even being involved with urban food production. However, there are opportunities in promoting urban regeneration, allowing nonplanning department control of some agricultural lands, and planning ahead for green space and agricultural space. Howe concluded that planning can have an important role in urban food production of particular types and at particular times. More generally, the planning barriers to urban food production tend to be political not physical. Howe also concluded that planners should see urban food production as an important instrument for promoting sustainable development.

Keywords: Food security, sustainability, urban food production, urban planning.

136. Moore, S. 2006. Forgotten roots of the green city: subsistence gardening in Columbus, Ohio, 1900-1940. Urban Geography. 27(2): 174–192.

Describes how two discourses, the urban narrative and crisis narrative, have divided concepts of urban (city) and rural (nature). The author conducted a literature review of urban gardening in Columbus, Ohio, from 1900 to 1940 to show that gardening has always been part of the cityscape despite common perceptions that subsistence gardening has only been practiced as a means of crisis mediation. This article raises questions about the tendency for urban activists and planners to overlook historical practices within a given jurisdiction.

Keywords: Community gardens, environmental history, gardening, subsistence, urban food production.

137. Stuart, S.M. 2005. Lifting spirits: creating gardens in California domestic violence shelters. In: Barlett, P.F., ed. Urban place: reconnecting with the natural world. Cambridge, MA: MIT Press: 61–68.

Stuart described Project GROW (Gardens for Respect, Opportunity, and Wellness), a pilot project in California that provided 1,500 women and children living in domestic violence shelters during the late 1990s and early 2000s with opportunities to participate in community gardening and related activities, such as food preservation and cooking workshops. Project GROW grew out of research in the field of horticultural therapy that showed that being around and working with plants can positively affect people's mental outlook and improve self-esteem. Stuart conducted an evaluation of the project, interviewing 60 women and 21 children who participated in the program, as well as 18 project administrators. Major impacts of the project listed by participants included improvement in emotional well-being (66 percent), educational benefits (34 percent), and access to fresh produce (16 percent). Adult participants from rural backgrounds stated that gardening evoked childhood memories and cultural and family traditions from earlier days. This was especially important for immigrant women, but also held true for American-born women who had grown up in rural parts of the United States. Participants also noted that gardening offered opportunities for them to connect with other residents, particularly those from other cultures. Stuart concluded that gardening programs are important as much for the psychological and social benefits they provide as for improving access to fresh, nutritional food.

Keywords: Community gardens, gardening, human health, identity, social benefits, urban food production, well-being.

138. Svendsen, E.S. 2009. Cultivating resilience: urban stewardship as a means to improving health and well-being. In: Campbell, L.; Wiesen, A., eds. Restorative commons: creating health and well-being through urban landscapes. Gen. Tech. Rep. NRS-P-39. Newtown Square, PA: U.S. Department of Agriculture, Forest Service, Northern Research Station: 54–72.

Svendsen argued that over the past few decades, urban planning discourse has shifted from one emphasizing public health (the "Sanitary City") to ecosystem health (the "Sustainable City"). Svendsen suggested that the discourse on sustainability needs to continue to bring in public health connections, focusing in particular on links between environmental stewardship and individual and collective well-being. She argued that there is a distinction between passive and interactive ways of engaging with the environment, and that active stewardship differs from passive interaction in that it involves responsibilities, rights, and preferences. She tested whether there is a link between stewardship and well-being through studying 3,000 community garden groups in New York City. The majority of individuals interviewed stated that they participated in the gardens to beautify their neighborhoods, to create or improve green space, and to create a place where they could relax and feel at peace. Only 40 percent stated that they gardened for food or to contribute to economic development. Other important motivations included teaching their children and passing on a legacy to others. Svendsen concluded that planners need to recognize that green urban designs require a complementary social network to be sustainable.

Keywords: Community gardens, economic benefits, green space, human health, social benefits, stewardship, sustainability, urban food production, urban planning, well-being.

139. Thompson, C.W. 2002. Urban open space in the 21st century. Landscape and Urban Planning. 60: 59–72.

This article looks at how open spaces can be defined in ways that accommodate the value differences that exist in a heterogeneous society. Today's urban parks reflect the values of late 19th-century planners who saw parks as places for bringing together people of all walks of life so as to create a unified democratic Nation. However, this vision carried with it specific views about what was considered appropriate behavior in such places, focusing on nature as a backdrop rather than nature as a place where people could have tactile interactions with the biophysical environment. Thompson observed that carefully tended environments do not appeal to everyone, and there is a need to recognize the value of "waste lots." In particular, she noted that these are places where children can "break sticks and branches" and "learn about the physical properties of things by testing them to destruction" (Thompson 2002: 67). She pointed to community gardens as a place where interactive engagement with nature can happen, and stressed their importance for human well-being and psychological growth. She argued for urban planning to include more "loose-fit" places, which "allow for a variety of functions and which are often undersigned, unregulated spaces" (Thompson 2002: 69), in their repertoire of green spaces. These would not only provide children with places to test their environment but they would also be ecologically appropriate, mimicking cycles of growth and decay. At a larger landscape scale, she called for rethinking the impending transformation of the countryside into spaces where productive uses are not permitted. She concluded that there is a need for spaces where humans can tactilely interact with natural processes.

Keywords: Green space, urban planning, well-being.

140. Von Hassell, M. 2005. Community gardens in New York City: place, community, and individuality. In: Barlett, P.F., ed. Urban place: reconnecting with the natural world. Cambridge, MA: MIT Press: 91–116.

Provides a short history of the community garden movement in the United States, with emphasis on recent efforts to prevent the destruction of community gardens in the lower east side of New York City. Von Hassell distinguished between two major eras in urban garden initiatives in the United States. The first took place between 1894 and 1945 and was largely government initiated. In this era, urban gardens were viewed primarily as sources of food for the poor, tools for reducing social tensions and improving psychological well-being, and a means to promote self-reliance and a strong work ethic. The second era features grass-roots community gardens, and began in the 1970s. Von Hassell argued that community gardens are places where people are active participants in processes of growth and decay. Far more than mere green spaces, they offer a wide range of benefits including social interaction, fresh and nutritious produce, physical exercise, as well as psychological benefits and opportunities for learning, teaching, and engaging with nature.

Keywords: Community gardens, gardening, human health, social benefits, urban food production, urban planning, well-being.

Acknowledgments

We thank Jay Bolthouse, John C. Dwyer, and Jenna Tilt for their insightful comments and suggestions for revising the peer review draft of this manuscript. Funding for the project was provided by the USDA Forest Service Northern Research Station in Burlington, Vermont, and the USDA Forest Service Pacific Northwest Research Station in Portland, Oregon, under contract AG63PX080095.

Appendix—List of Keywords Used in Annotations

Numbers are citation numbers, not page numbers.

biodiversity—54, 88, 109, 110, 114

community gardens—9, 136, 137, 138, 140

conservation—10, 34, 110, 113, 126

crime—77, 87, 92, 121, 131

cultural ecology—69, 71, 72, 73, 74, 75, 76

cultural practices—1, 2, 3, 4, 5, 6, 7, 10, 11, 12, 13, 14, 15, 18, 33, 95, 115, 119, 125

ecological knowledge—3, 5, 10, 39, 88, 71, 111

ecological restoration—73, 74, 81, 82, 86, 93, 110, 126

economic benefits—123, 124, 128, 138

edible plants—20, 21, 22, 23, 24, 26, 27, 28, 29, 30, 31, 34, 50

environmental health—39, 100, 101, 102, 103, 104, 105

environmental history—77, 132, 136

environmental justice—6, 77, 78, 80, 81, 82, 86, 107

environmental psychology—70, 87, 88, 89, 90, 91, 92, 93, 96, 97, 98, 99, 121, 133

ethnobotany—1, 2, 4

ethnoecology—1, 2, 4, 10

ethnomedicine—1, 2, 4

food security—19, 36, 37, 42, 43, 44, 46, 47, 48, 51, 53, 54, 55, 56, 57, 58, 59, 60, 61, 62, 63, 64, 66, 67, 68, 135

fruit sharing—9, 36, 37, 42, 43, 44, 46, 47, 48, 49, 51, 52, 53, 56, 58, 59, 61, 62, 63, 64, 66, 67, 68

gardening—9, 69, 70, 72, 73, 74, 75, 76, 80, 90, 96, 136, 137, 140

gathering—11, 12, 13, 14, 15, 16, 17, 18, 19, 85, 120

gleaning—9, 36, 37, 42, 43, 44, 46, 47, 48, 49, 51, 52, 53, 56, 58, 59, 62, 63, 64, 67, 68

green space—88, 107, 134, 138, 139

heavy metals—100, 103, 104, 105